How to think like

EINSTEIN

....

DANIEL SMITH

By the same author:

How to Think Like Sherlock
How to Think Like Steve Jobs
How to Think Like Mandela

How to think like
EINSTEIN

. . . .

DANIEL SMITH

Michael O'Mara Books Limited

For Charlotte

First published in Great Britain in 2014 by
Michael O'Mara Books Limited
9 Lion Yard
Tremadoc Road
London SW4 7NQ

A CIP catalogue record for this book is available from the British Library.

Papers used by Michael O'Mara Books Limited are natural, recyclable
products made from wood grown in sustainable forests. The manufacturing
processes conform to the environmental regulations of the country of origin.

ISBN: 978-1-78243-215-9 in hardback print format
ISBN: 978-1-78243-311-8 in paperback print format
ISBN: 978-1-78243-269-2 in e-book format

1 2 3 4 5 6 7 8 9 10

Printed and bound by CPI Group (UK) Ltd, Croydon, CR0 4YY

Designed and typeset by Envy Design Ltd

www.mombooks.com

Contents

Introduction

'Certainly he was a great savant, but beyond that
he was also a pillar of human conscience at a
moment when so many civilizing values
seemed to be in the balance.'

PABLO CASALS

'Genius' is a much over-used term, but Albert
Einstein is one of the few who is doubtless
worthy of the epithet. Indeed, his very name has
become commonly accepted shorthand for the word.
It may reasonably be argued that there has been no
more important and influential a figure in the history
of science, and it requires a particular type of genius to
inhabit such a role.

Yet, for several years he ploughed a lonely furrow as
a part-time theoretical physicist with a day job at the
Swiss Patent Office. It was not until he was in his mid-
twenties that he burst spectacularly on to the scientific
scene. In an extraordinary outpouring of intellectual
insight, he delivered a series of papers in the first two
decades of the twentieth century that overhauled our

understanding of the universe – from the sub-atomic level to the cosmos as a whole. He laid the groundwork for modern quantum mechanics (although he questioned the concept for the duration of his life) as well as producing first his special theory and then the general theory of relativity, which together redefined the very nature of time and space. As such, he is the forefather of the twin pillars of modern physics.

Yet still he refused to take his foot off the gas. As he would tell his son in 1930: 'Life is like riding a bicycle. To keep your balance you must keep moving.' So it was that he devoted his later years to the search for a unified field theory. Perhaps only Newton could claim to have had equal impact over such a breadth of scientific thought. Today we can see the evidence of his ideas all around us, in everything from our televisions and cameras to GPS systems, fibre optics and, more esoterically, our understanding of the nature of black holes.

A theorist rather than an experimentalist, his intellectualism was underpinned by an unfaltering belief in the individual's right to freedom of thought and spirit. Einstein was a true revolutionary, prepared to challenge and overturn ideas that had been considered fact for centuries. He believed nothing was immune to reappraisal, and his accomplishments demonstrated how we should never be content to take anything for granted.

But Einstein was not only an extraordinary scientific thinker. He was a humanitarian who detested war and tried to stem the proliferation of hitherto unimaginably destructive weapons that his work had in part made possible. The spectre of the atomic bomb, and his unintended role in its creation, haunted him. As Pablo Picasso noted in 1964: 'Every positive value has its price in negative terms ... The genius of Einstein leads to Hiroshima.' It was a blot on a lifetime devoted to fighting authoritarianism, promoting personal freedom and selflessly standing up to those who posed a threat to such ideals.

Furthermore, he was a *bona fide* superstar in the days when global celebrity was a far harder thing to achieve than it is now – especially if you were a dishevelled academic and not a recording star or matinee idol. He was instantly recognizable to millions who had not the least understanding of the intricacies of his scientific theories. Even now, the image of the tousle-haired 'mad professor' poking his tongue out at the camera is familiar across the globe. He had a caustic wit and a talent for delivering *bon mots*. He was also a man of enormous personal complexity. Just as he could express enormous empathy for humanity at large, he could treat those closest to him with breathtaking disdain that at times bordered on the cruel. He was a great man, but – like many great men – had significant flaws.

What this book is *not* is a quick guide to Einstein's science. Once, when asked to explain relativity in a sentence, he replied it would take him three days to give a short answer. If you want to understand the intricacies of relativity or of light quanta or any of the other myriad subjects he theorized upon, you can do no better than read his original papers. While some of the material is of a complexity not for the faint-hearted, much of it is eminently accessible. Einstein prided himself on refining his theories so that the underlying concepts might make sense to anybody.

Instead, *How to Think Like Einstein* aims to explore how he went about his work, to investigate the disparate components of his personality and to look at some of the key influences that informed his world view. As with all of the subjects in the *How to Think Like …* series, he was a global icon with talents and skills that set him aside from the rest of us. But he was also an individual born with faults and frailties with which we can all identify. It is my hope that this text will reveal a little of what made him both great but also reassuringly human.

Landmarks in a Remarkable Life

1879   Albert Einstein is born on 14 March in Ulm, Germany, to a Jewish family.

1880   The Einsteins move to Munich where Albert's father and uncle establish a gas and electrical supply business.

1881   A sister for Albert, Maria (known as Maja), is born.

1892   Albert opts not to attend his bar mitzvah.

1894   Einstein's parents and sisters move to Italy for his father's work. Albert moves in with relatives in Munich while he finishes his schooling, but joins his parents before he has graduated.

1895   After failing to secure a place at Zurich Polytechnic aged sixteen, Einstein goes to further his studies in Aarau, where he resides with the Winteler family. He writes his first (unpublished) scientific paper.

1896   Surrenders his German citizenship and wins a place at Zurich Polytechnic. There he meets his future wife, Mileva Marić.

1899   Applies for Swiss citizenship.

1900   Secures his teaching diploma from Zurich but fails to secure a job at the Polytechnic.

1901   Has a scientific paper published for the first time. It appears in *Annalen der Physik*. He receives his Swiss citizenship.

1902   Marić gives birth to Einstein's illegitimate daughter, Lieserl. Einstein begins work at the Bern Patent Office.

1903   Einstein and Marić marry. The Olympia Academy is formed in Bern by Einstein and two friends. All historical records of Lieserl end – it is probable that she is put up for adoption.

1904   Marić gives birth to a son, Hans Albert.

Landmarks in a Remarkable Life

1905   The *annus mirabilis*, in which Einstein completes four papers that re-write the foundations of physics. He also formulates the equation $E = mc^2$.

1906   Receives his doctorate from the University of Zurich.

1907   Turns his attentions to formulating the general theory of relativity, in the process discovering the principle of equivalence.

1908   Becomes an unsalaried *Privatdozent* at the University of Bern and begins lecturing.

1909   Appointed Extraordinary Professor for Theoretical Physics at the University of Zurich.

1910   Marić gives birth to a second son, Eduard.

1911   Takes up a professorship in Prague. He also attends the first Solvay Conference in Brussels.

1912   Begins an affair with his Berlin-based cousin, Elsa Löwenthal. He returns to Zurich to take up a professorship and begins working with Marcel Grossmann on the mathematics necessary for his general theory of relativity.

1913   Max Planck and Walther Nernst woo Einstein to Berlin with the promise of a professorship at the university and membership of the Prussian Academy of Sciences. He takes up this position the following year.

1914   Einstein and Marić separate, and she leaves Berlin for Zurich with her two sons. Meanwhile, a politicized Einstein promotes his belief in pacifism as the First World War begins.

1915   Works with W. J. de Haas on investigations into the gyromagnetic effect. By November Einstein completes his general theory of relativity, which he outlines over four lectures at the Prussian Academy of Sciences.

1916   His paper entitled 'The Formal Foundation of the General Theory of Relativity' is published in the *Annalen der Physik*. By the end of the year he finishes *On the Special and General Theory of Relativity, A Popular Account*.

1917   Takes over management of Berlin's Kaiser Wilhelm Institute for Physics. Also outlines his theory of the cosmological constant, which he will come to consider his 'biggest idiocy'.

1918 Rejects a return to teaching in Switzerland. The First World War comes to an end.

1919 Einstein divorces Marić in February and marries Elsa in June. In May, the astronomer Arthur Stanley Eddington proves Einstein's theory of light deflection in the gravitational field of the sun (a key component of the general theory) using observations during a solar eclipse. Einstein's fame spreads around the world.

1920 Meets Niels Bohr, the celebrated quantum theorist, for the first time. Within Germany, Einstein finds himself a focus of increasing anti-Semitic sentiment.

1921 Spends two months touring the USA (his first visit to the country) with Chaim Weizmann, a Zionist who will become Israel's president. Einstein's motivation is to raise money for the prospective Hebrew University of Jerusalem.

1922 Awarded the Nobel Prize in Physics for 1921, for his services to theoretical physics, and especially for his discovery of the law of the photoelectric effect.

1924   Work with Indian physicist Satyendra Nath Bose results in the prediction of Bose–Einstein condensates, a state of matter not created under laboratory conditions until 1995.

1925   Formulation of the Bose–Einstein statistics, an important component of quantum mechanics. Einstein also joins the board of governors of the newly opened Hebrew University of Jerusalem.

1927   Debates quantum theory with Niels Bohr at the fifth Solvay Conference in Brussels.

1928   Spends much of the year housebound by illness. Helen Dukas starts work as his secretary and she will become his devoted protector until his death.

1929   Builds his beloved summerhouse at Caputh near Potsdam.

1930   Calls for global disarmament. He makes a second visit to the USA, staying at the California Institute of Technology (CalTech), Pasadena.

1931   Returns to Europe in March but goes back to the USA in December. He comes to the conclusion that his cosmological constant is incorrect.

1932   Travels to the USA in December unaware he will never return to Germany.

1933   Cuts his ties with Germany after Adolf Hitler comes to power. Following a brief return to Europe (when he stays in Belgium, Switzerland and the UK), he goes back to the USA to take up a post at the Institute for Advanced Study in Princeton, New Jersey.

1934   A collection of non-scientific works, *The World As I See It*, is published.

1935   Publication of the Einstein–Podolsky–Rosen Paradox (the EPR Paper). Einstein and Elsa move to 112 Mercer Street in Princeton.

1936   Elsa dies on 20 December after a long illness.

1938   Publishes *The Evolution of Physics* in collaboration with Leopold Infeld.

1939   Signs a letter to US President Franklin D. Roosevelt warning of the threat of an atomic bomb shortly before the Second World War commences.

1940   Becomes an American citizen, while retaining his Swiss citizenship.

1942   The US government commences the Manhattan Project to develop an atomic bomb. Einstein is not directly involved, having been deemed a security risk.

1943   Undertakes work for the US Navy into highly explosive materials.

1944   A copy of Einstein's 1905 paper 'On the Electrodynamics of Moving Bodies' is auctioned for US$6 million.

1945   Responds to the end of the Second World War and the dropping of atom bombs on the Japanese cities of Hiroshima and Nagasaki by saying: 'The war is won, but the peace is not.'

1946   Renews his calls for the creation of a supranational government and heads up the Emergency Committee of Atomic Scientists, which seeks the peaceful use of nuclear energy.

1948   Mileva Marić dies on 4 August. Einstein is diagnosed with an aneurysm of the abdominal aorta and undergoes surgery.

1949   *Autobiographical Notes*, a review of his career written three years earlier, is published.

1950   *Out of My Later Years*, a collection of non-scientific essays and speeches, is published.

1951   Maja, Einstein's sister, dies on 25 June.

1952   Rejects the opportunity to succeed Chaim Weizmann as President of Israel.

1955   Agrees to sign what becomes known as the Russell–Einstein Manifesto, the founding document of the Pugwash movement, concerned with science and world affairs.

1955   Dies in hospital in Princeton on 18 April, aged 76.

Life is a Marathon, Not a Sprint

'I never think of the future. It comes soon enough.'

ALBERT EINSTEIN, 1930

For any parents intent on hothousing their young child in a bid to guarantee their future success, Einstein provides an object lesson that genius may take a while to find its way into the open. One of his school teachers, a certain Dr Joseph Degenhart, even secured himself a place in the footnotes of history by errantly concluding of his wayward pupil that he would 'never get anywhere in life'.

Albert Einstein entered the world on 14 March 1879, born in the German city of Ulm to Jewish parents, Hermann and Pauline. A sister, Maria (known as Maja), followed two years later. As a Jew in late nineteenth-century Germany, Einstein was instantly cast into the role of the outsider, a status that not only informed his psyche but had a profound influence on how others treated him throughout his life.

His family was typically bourgeois. His father, a talented mathematician, worked in the burgeoning electricity industry but suffered badly from a lack of business acumen. There was, truth be told, little in the family background to suggest Albert was destined for greatness. He was a late developer when it came to speaking – so much so that the family maid rather cruelly nicknamed him 'the dopey one'. In addition, he suffered from a condition called *echolalia*, which led him to repeat phrases several times. While there is little evidence to suggest that Einstein suffered from autism to any significant degree (and indeed, there is much to support the notion that he didn't), his *echolalia* has led some to speculate that he was to some extent afflicted.

Furthermore, he was a daydreamer, which could make him seem a little distant, and he had few friends of his own age as a young child. However, when he was five Einstein had his 'road to Damascus moment'. If it was a pivotal event for him personally, it would prove no less so for mankind. Einstein was poorly at the time and was recuperating in bed when his father presented him with a gift to distract him – a compass. The way that the needle rooted out north without any mechanical intervention rendered the boy astonished. Einstein himself described the moment as leaving him cold and shivery (good for science but probably not ideal for an already sick child). Here was an object that showed with brilliant clarity the physical effects of an invisible force. From that moment on, Einstein was obsessed by the unseen forces that influence our universe.

It has become part of folklore that Einstein was not very bright at school, no doubt partly the result of Dr Degenhart's ill-advised utterance. However, Albert was, by most accounts, a very able student, especially in the field of maths. In that subject he was working to an academic level several years beyond his age. By the time he was twelve, he was, in his own words, 'thrilled to see that it was possible to find out truths by reasoning alone, without the help of any outside experience'. But while, like his father, he certainly had a talent for mathematics, no one was proffering him as a science visionary. When he attempted to gain a place at university aged sixteen (two years earlier than normal), his test results showed he had some catching up to do in several of his other subjects, including botany, literature and politics.

In order to get a place at the Zurich Polytechnic, he attended school in the Swiss town of Aarau and came second in his class. Again, he had proven himself a capable student but had hardly set the world alight. (Although his name is of course far better known to us than that of the pupil who beat him into first place.) When he graduated from the Polytechnic in 1900, he was an undistinguished fourth in his class of five. He then made unsuccessful attempts to win an academic position at Zurich and an assortment of other institutions. In 1901, after much frustration, he was forced to take the relatively lowly position of Technical Expert (Class 3) at the Swiss Patent Office in Bern.

It is chastening, then, to think that only four years later Einstein would produce a series of papers that turned the world of science on its head. Even more remarkably, he did it all under his own steam and in his spare time. Einstein would later suggest that it was perhaps his lack of speed off the mark that helped him achieve his later triumphs. He would reflect: ' ... I developed so slowly that I began to wonder about space and time only when I was already grown up.'

Yet even after he had shared his intellectual leaps forward with the rest of the world, it took several more years before he started to get the recognition he warranted. Extraordinarily, he only received his first junior professorship in 1909 – not only nine years after he had graduated, but fully four years after he had published his paper on the special theory of relativity and calculated that $E = mc^2$. Nor would a Nobel Prize be his, officially, until 1922.

All of which surely goes to prove that even for an intellect as stellar as Einstein's, slow and steady wins the race.

Be Curious

'I have no special talents. I am only
passionately curious.'

ALBERT EINSTEIN, 1952

For all that we may wonder at the intellectual processes that propelled Einstein to greatness, he himself seemed to believe that there was nothing so important as his relentless desire to find answers to the really big questions. As he wrote in a letter in his later years: 'My scientific work is motivated by an irresistible longing to understand the secrets of nature and by no other feelings.' To Alexander Moszkowski, a friend who published an early biography of him in 1920, Albert explained that it was his inner conviction that the development of science was mainly driven by the need to satisfy the longing for pure knowledge.

Crucially, he was also convinced that the answers were there, just waiting to be discovered. In 1938 he co-authored *The Evolution of Physics: The Growth of Ideas From Early Concepts to Relativity and Quanta*. In it, he would note that 'without the belief in the inner harmony of our world, there could be no science'. His certainty that the great mysteries of our world and the cosmos had rational solutions came to him at a relatively young age. By the time he was around twelve he was certain that nature could be interpreted through the application of mathematical structures, most of which he considered to be 'relatively simple' (though those of us without his innate grasp of maths and physics reserve the right to take some issue with that). It was an idea he expanded upon at the Herbert Spencer lecture he gave in Oxford in 1933:

> Our experience hitherto justifies us in believing that nature is the realization of the simplest conceivable mathematical ideas. I am convinced that we can discover by means of purely mathematical constructions the concepts and the laws connecting them with each other, which furnish the key to the understanding of natural phenomena.

Einstein was thus able to combine a sense of wonder at the world with a belief that he could come to understand what lay behind those wonders. The sickly infant who had marvelled at the seemingly mystical powers of the compass soon found his interests expanding to take in the mysteries of heat and electricity (no wonder, given that the family business was electricity generation). He grew up, too, in a period when science was just starting to come to terms with the physical reality of atoms and molecules (essentially, the unseen building blocks of the universe), while the emerging field of kinetic theory (the motion of particles within matter) was another major area of interest for him in his youth.

He had his heroes too, citing Galileo and Newton to Moszkowski as the two greatest creative geniuses that science had thrown up. Of these, it was arguably Newton who he most looked up to, an irony given that much of Einstein's work would throw into chaos many of the Newtonian 'realities' that the scientific world had accepted for over two centuries. Writing a foreword in 1931 to a reissue of Newton's 1704 work *Opticks*, Einstein said of him: 'In one person he combined the experimenter, the theorist, the mechanic, and, not the least, the artist of exposition.' He might have been describing himself, although there are those who would suggest that Einstein's skills as an experimenter lagged some way behind those of his eminent predecessor.

He was, though, quite as great a theorist and this was in part due to his conviction that a theory should be boiled down to its simplest state. As he would note in the 1940s, a theory is increasingly impressive the simpler its premises and the greater variety of things that it encompasses. It was his belief that, when one has removed the complex mathematics that may be required to express it, a good theory should be uncomplicated enough to describe that even a child may understand it. The revelation of fundamental truths through an attachment to simplicity had great currency in the age of modernism. Ponder the words of the epoch's greatest artist, Pablo Picasso, who held that it had taken him four years to learn to paint like Raphael but a lifetime to paint like a child.

It of course helped his progress that Einstein was by nature an independent spirit, unafraid to branch out on his own. Here was a youth who felt equipped at the age of fifteen to wave off his family as they left for Pavia in northern Italy in order to pursue new business interests after his father's lighting company went bust. Then he had the gumption to unilaterally up sticks and join them under his own steam, vowing never to return to Germany and determined to renounce his German citizenship. He was also confident enough to apply for a Polytechnic place two years early. Always something of an outsider, he seemed to feel little need to conform – a trait that would serve him well in his career.

Furthermore, he benefited from his family's background in electricity generation: he worked for his father at various points and had access to equipment that offered him practical opportunities to explore some of his early physics fascinations. Then there was the distinct streak of arrogance that gave him the impetus to follow remarkable new directions that a more callow youth might have feared to explore. Consider, for instance, his first scientific paper, written in 1901. Although it was a piece of juvenilia lacking finesse, the paper fearlessly critiqued the work of two of the greatest physicists of the age, Ludwig Boltzmann and Paul Drude.

Yet perhaps this did not register as arrogance to Einstein, for whom one's very identity was defined by one's thoughts and ideas. 'The essential in the being of a man of my type,' he wrote in 1946, 'lies precisely in *what* he thinks and *how* he thinks, not in what he does or suffers.' Einstein was not critiquing his apparent elders and betters for the sake of it, then, but because he felt he had no choice but to point out errors that he felt were restraining scientific progress.

And just as sometimes it is better to travel than to arrive, perhaps it was more pleasurable for Einstein to explore his curiosity than it was even to find answers. As he put it to his friend Heinrich Zangger in 1918: 'The mainspring of scientific thought is not an external goal toward which one must strive, but the pleasure of thinking.'

Follow Your Intuition

'All great achievements of science must start from intuitive knowledge, namely, in axioms, from which deductions are then made … Intuition is the necessary condition for the discovery of such axioms.'

ALBERT EINSTEIN, 1920

Allied to his unstinting curiosity was a deep faith in his own intuition. It is safe to say that all of his greatest discoveries were the result of feats of the mind, which he then sought to prove evidentially. That is not to say that this is the only way to exercise one's intellect. In science and across all other academic disciplines, there are plenty of major figures who have gathered evidence and from that evidence reached new conclusions. Einstein, though, worked by envisioning certain scenarios in more of an abstract manner and then set out to prove or disprove his hypothesis. This was how intuition fuelled his great leaps forward. As he told G. S. Viereck – a German-American writer, poet and journalist and, it would turn out, Nazi sympathizer – in a 1929 interview: 'I believe in intuitions and inspirations ... I sometimes *feel* that I am right. I do not *know* that I am.'

It was an idea he had fleshed out ten years earlier in the essay 'Induction and Deduction in Physics':

The truly great advances in our understanding of nature originated in a way almost diametrically opposed to induction. The intuitive grasp of the essentials of a large complex of facts leads the scientist to the postulation of a hypothetical basic law or laws. From these laws, he derives his conclusions.

Needless to say, it was not the case that Einstein saw no value in inductive reasoning – in other words, the arrival at general principles from the consideration of facts gathered by experimentation. Indeed, he recognized that all scientists to a lesser or greater degree blend inductive and deductive methods. He himself built his hypotheses around fixed points anchored in an experimentally proven basis. Einstein admired the way that the inductive method allowed single facts to be 'selected and grouped together so that the laws that connect them become clearly apparent'. These laws then made possible the formulation of more general laws 'until a more or less uniform system for the available individual facts has been established'.

So he did not simply pluck theories out of thin air – there had to be an empirical dimension to his thought processes. But he launched off in directions unseen by others, his intuition pushing him towards previously unimagined conclusions. It was by no means a foolproof approach. He did not hit upon a general theory of relativity each time he sat at his desk; his intuition would lead him down countless cul-de-sacs. But it only takes one major discovery to mark out a life as exceptional, and Einstein could stake a claim to a good many more than one.

There has long been controversy over the extent to which Einstein was influenced by a test conducted in 1887, known as the Michelson–Morley experiment, when he was formulating his special theory of relativity. Whether or not he was remains moot but a comment he made in relation to the experiment is instructive in his faith in a good, old-fashioned hunch: 'I was pretty much convinced of the validity of the principle before I knew of this experiment and its results.'

In modern usage, intuition can suggest a sort of glorified or inspired bit of guesswork. A gut feeling that happens to be right but with indeterminate origins. Einstein did not see it in this light, though. For him, intuition had sources that might not be immediately clear but which ultimately stemmed from a previously acquired accumulation of knowledge and thought. He wrote to one Dr H. L. Gordon in 1949: 'A new idea comes suddenly and in a rather intuitive way. But intuition is nothing but the outcome of earlier intellectual experience.' Intuition, then, was not the thunderbolt of genius we might like to imagine but instead a considered philosophical approach to thinking.

See the World
Differently

'Imagination is more important than knowledge.
Knowledge is limited. Imagination encircles the world.'

ALBERT EINSTEIN, 1929

Going hand in hand with his trust in intuition was an unshakeable faith in the power of the imagination. It was this that allowed Einstein to take knowledge and to reconfigure it in totally original ways. He had the imagination (and the courage to give it a free rein) to see the world differently to anyone who had preceded him. As Nobel physicist Arthur Compton would note: 'Einstein is great because he has shown us our world in truer perspective and has helped us to understand a little more clearly how we are related to the universe around us.'

He then had the necessary skills to communicate his unique view of things to others. While Einstein's writings inevitably present a few challenges, for those with a moderate level of relevant background knowledge it is eminently possible to follow how he reshaped centuries of scientific wisdom.

When there was talk of him taking up a new academic post at the University of Prague in 1910, a large number of his students at Zurich were moved to sign a petition that they hoped would persuade the university authorities to retain him. 'Professor Einstein has an amazing talent for presenting the most difficult problems of theoretical physics so clearly and so comprehensibly,' they wrote, 'that it is a great delight for us to follow his lectures, and he is so good at establishing a perfect rapport with his audience.' He was, then, a visionary who could communicate his ideas – a rare gift indeed.

It is impossible to discern exactly what it was that gave him his extraordinary vision, but we have a few clues. It is certain, for instance, that Einstein – unlike the great majority of us – did not think verbally. 'I very rarely think in words at all,' he once stated. 'A thought comes, and I may try to express it in words afterwards.' So if he wasn't thinking in words, what was it that flashed across his mind?

It was as if his thoughts had a physical reality that eludes most of us. Contributing to Jacques Hadamard's remarkable 1945 work on mathematics, *The Mathematician's Mind: The Psychology of Invention in the Mathematical Field*, Einstein explained that 'the words or the language, as they are written or spoken, do not seem to play any role in my mechanism of thought'. He then described 'psychical entities which seem to serve as elements in thought' that were 'more or less clear images which can be "voluntarily" reproduced and combined … The above-mentioned elements,' he went on, 'are, in my case, of visual and some of muscular type.' It is a remarkably visceral description.

Allied to this non-verbal thought process was a

profound connection with the language of mathematics – a language that he believed held the key to the secrets of the natural world. He had the ability to 'see' equations, with one of his students describing how where he saw an abstract formula, Einstein could grasp its physical manifestation.

It is possible, though far from proven, that this skill was the result of a distinctive brain composition. In 1999, a neurobiological team led by Sandra Witelson at McMaster University in Hamilton, Canada, published a paper on the anatomy of Einstein's brain. Working largely from photographs, the team concluded that Einstein's parietal lobes – the bits of the brain associated with mathematical, visual and spatial cognition – were some fifteen per cent wider than the brains of a normative population sample. (Although, intriguingly, Einstein's total brain size was at the low end of average for a modern human.) Several years later, Dean Falk, an anthropologist at Florida State University in Tallahassee, speculated that a distinctive pattern of grooves and ridges in the parietal regions might have been responsible for Einstein's ability to conceptualize physics problems.

That Einstein thought predominantly in images and sensations and that he could bring a physical reality to abstract mathematical constructs fuelled his great imaginative leaps. But there were other aspects to his unique frame of perception. For example, his hunger for simple explanations to great problems was fed by, and fed into, a desire to retain a childlike (as opposed to childish) wonder at the world. He grasped the importance of retaining this outlook when he noted in 1921: 'Studying, and striving for truth and beauty in general, is a sphere in which we are allowed to be children throughout life.'

There was also a desire to take apparently disparate spokes of the scientific wheel and trace how they come together. In other words, where others would most likely see disconnects, his mind thrived on trying to find connections. He once wrote to his great friend Marcel Grossmann to explain: 'It is a glorious feeling to discover the unity of a set of phenomena that seem at first to be completely separate.'

It should also be noted that Einstein saw himself not in the narrow terms of 'scientist'. He once famously asserted: 'The greatest scientists are artists as well.' The implication was that big scientific developments require the same skill, vision and creativity that might have been found in any of his cultural heroes, from Mozart or Bach to Tolstoy or Shaw. At the core of any great artist is a formidable imagination, and Einstein would tell Viereck: 'I'm enough of an artist to draw freely on my imagination.'

THOUGHT EXPERIMENTS

'What if one were to run after a ray of light? . . .
What if one were riding on the beam? . . . If one were
to run fast enough, would it no longer move at all? . . .
What is the "velocity of light"?'

ALBERT EINSTEIN, 1916

Einstein was arguably history's greatest exponent of the thought experiment (in German, *Gedankenexperiment*). But what exactly is a thought experiment? In broad terms, it is a test devised in the imagination to realize the outcome of an idea or hypothesis for which there is an absence of physical proof. It is a device with a noble heritage amongst scientists and philosophers: such notable names as René Descartes, Galileo Galilei, Gottfried Leibniz and Isaac Newton have all made use of it in their work.

The quotation above recalls a thought experiment that first occupied Einstein's mind when he was a green sixteen-year-old. What would it be like, he wondered, to ride alongside a light beam? He pondered the question for the next ten years and his conclusions were instrumental in formulating the special theory of relativity. Just what it would be like to ride alongside a light beam is enough to boggle the mind when someone else puts the idea in your head, but for the young Einstein to not only devise the specifics of the conundrum but then to wrestle with the implications was an achievement of quite extraordinary levels.

There were more thought experiments of equal importance to follow. Also in pursuit of the special theory, he imagined a situation in which a moving train was simultaneously struck by lightning at both its ends and then considered how such an event might appear to a stationary observer on the railway embankment and to someone aboard the train. The results at which he arrived turned his (and our) understanding of time upside down.

His third great thought experiment (which came to him one quiet day in his office) involved putting a subject in an enclosed elevator-like box and allowing them to free fall. The subject, he came to realize, would have no idea whether they were in the grip of a gravitational field or in gravity-free deep space. It was an insight that informed the development of the general theory.

These were just a few of the many thought experiments that he conducted over his career. Others had significant influence, such as one involving a keg of unstable gunpowder, which in quantum terms may be deemed to be in a state somewhere between unexploded and exploded (a contravention of the 'real state of affairs', according to Einstein). Schrödinger acknowledged that this imaginary keg was instrumental in the development of his own 'cat', surely the most famous conceptual feline in history.

Most of Einstein's flights of intellectual fancy inevitably failed to reap the rich rewards of those described here, but all helped hone his understanding of the physical world. They are also evidence of how Einstein harnessed his formidable imagination in the interests of science. As he described it: 'It is a sudden illumination, almost a rapture. Later, to be sure, intelligence analyses and experiments confirm or invalidate the intuition. But initially there is a great leap forward of the imagination.'

Seek Out
Like Minds

'I am a horse for single harness, not cut
out for tandem or team work.'

ALBERT EINSTEIN, 1930

As the quotation on the previous page suggests, Einstein was a man who, for the large part of his life, worked alone. His greatest discoveries were mostly solitary achievements. That said, he had an uncanny knack of rooting out intellectual and philosophical soulmates who, even if they had limited direct impact on his work, played important roles in his overall development.

Take the example of Max Talmud. It was the custom of the Einsteins to invite Talmud, a poor local medical student, to a meal each Thursday, beginning when Einstein was about ten years old. Talmud, eleven years Albert's senior, recalled rarely seeing his young companion with any friends his own age, yet the two of them immediately hit it off.

Talmud fed Einstein's insatiable hunger for knowledge with a regular supply of titles from his scientific library. To begin with, it was maths that underpinned their friendship, with Einstein gleefully showing his progress in problem-solving each week. Before long, Talmud recognized that his protégé had surpassed him in understanding. At that stage, he introduced more philosophical texts, from Kant to David Hume and Ernst Mach. They discussed probing questions such as what it is possible to know about reality, in the process providing Einstein with a grounding that informed much of his life's work. Having chanced upon Talmud, Einstein had recognized a kindred spirit and had used the friendship to aid his intellectual growth. Their paths diverged after a while and the two lost contact, though Talmud would relate how the relationship was briefly rekindled after a gap of almost twenty years.

When Einstein moved to Aarau for his studies in 1895, he again showed his gift for latching on to 'his kind of people' while lodging with the Winteler family. Jost, the family patriarch, took Albert under his wing and the two spent hours discussing politics. A liberal, Jost's deep-seated suspicion of nationalism and militarism resonated with his young charge. Over time he had a profound influence on Einstein's politics: shadows of Winteler Senior may be seen throughout Einstein's liberal, left-leaning, democratic and federalist outlooks.

Then there were the alliances he formed with other scientists. At Zurich Polytechnic he met Michele Besso, probably the single most important friend of his life, who doubled as a sounding board for Einstein's scientific ideas. Another Zurich alumnus and close friend was Marcel Grossmann, whose mathematical skills Einstein plundered on his way to the general theory. Also from the Polytechnic was his future wife, Mileva Marić, whose relationship with Albert bloomed in an atmosphere of mutual intellectual admiration.

While it is generally true that Einstein worked best on his own, he never lost sight of the dangers of working in a vacuum. Having produced works of incalculable value at a relatively young age and then been lauded by not only the scientific community but the world at large, it would have been easy for a man of such a naturally solitary bent to have believed he needed no one else. Thankfully, he never succumbed to such vanity.

So it was that he formed plenty of temporary alliances to supplement fruitful relationships nurtured over decades (many of which had to be navigated through periods of professional disagreement). As a result, he completed important work with such notable names as Peter Bergmann, Satyendra Nath Bose, Wander Johannes de Haas, Leopold Infeld, Boris Podolsky, Nathan Rosen and Leó Szilárd. There was also an immediate affinity with Marie Curie, who in 1917 wrote:

> I was able to appreciate the clarity of his mind, the breadth of his information, and the profundity of his knowledge ... One has every right to build the greatest hopes on him and to see in him one of the leading theoreticians of the future.

Nor was Einstein content with admitting to his circle only those who broadly agreed with him. As a challenger of certainties himself, he happily engaged with those ready and able to question his own apparent 'truths'. Most notably, he engaged in ferocious intellectual sparring with Niels Bohr, the Danish godfather of quantum physics, while simultaneously forming a profound bond. In 1920 he wrote to Bohr: 'Not often in my life has a person given me such joy by his presence as you have.' Max Born should also be added to the list of those who became great friends while taking up an opposed scientific position (as with Bohr, in support of quantum theory). And Erwin Schrödinger, as we have already seen, was another with whom Einstein hit it off. Albert was a keen supporter of Schrödinger's work and vice versa, despite regular stand-offs over scientific interpretation.

For a man who by his own admission could be difficult, Einstein had a talent for maintaining relationships across class, race and gender. Friends he made as an uncelebrated young man lasted a lifetime, while there were also profound connections with a disparate array of (sometimes quite unexpected) figures once he had become a global icon. In 1914, for instance, he met and conversed deeply with the Indian Nobel Literature laureate, Rabindranath Tagore. An intense exchange of letters with Sigmund Freud followed in the 1930s. There was also an unlikely friendship with Elisabeth of Bavaria, wife of Albert I and Queen of the Belgians. The monarch and the scientist first met in the late 1920s and kept up a colourful correspondence full of shared confidences over many years.

And what of arguably Einstein's most 'showbiz'

acquaintance, Charlie Chaplin? It may not have been the deepest of bonds but they met in the early 1930s when the Little Tramp was the undisputed king of Hollywood. At the time, they were perhaps the only two men on the planet who could rival each other in fame. Both, in their own ways, had fundamentally altered how people saw the world. They also shared a political leaning towards the left and Einstein had let it be known that he had long wanted to meet the film star. The pair hit it off and appeared alongside each other on the red carpet following the premiere of *City Lights* in 1931. If Einstein had greater insight into the celestial, Chaplin had the edge when it came to stardom. Surveying the baying throng, he wryly noted: 'They cheer me because they all understand me, and they cheer you because no one understands you.' Einstein is then reported to have asked him, 'What does it all mean?' To which Chaplin replied, 'Nothing.'

Chaplin clearly realized the difference between uncritical adulation and genuine engagement with people who 'get' you. Einstein's track record of friendships suggests he understood that the same rules applies in his world, too.

THE OLYMPIA ACADEMY

Of all the estimable academic institutions of which Einstein was a member over his lifetime, there was none as close to his heart as the *Akademie Olympia* (Olympia Academy) that he and a few like-minded associates founded in Bern, Switzerland, in 1902.

The existence of the Academy came about as the result of an advertisement Einstein placed in a local newspaper, *Anzeiger der Stadt Bern*, in late 1901. He was in the city hoping to get a job at the patent office but for the time being found himself at a loose end. Therefore, he offered his services as a tutor in maths and physics for a modest fee (the first session was even for free).

The notice caught the eye of Maurice Solovine, a Romanian philosophy student keen to expand his knowledge of physics. The two agreed to meet. However, rather than Einstein covering the scientific topics he had planned, the two chatted amiably across a broad range of subjects. Einstein quickly realized that he was less interested in teaching Solovine and taking his money than he was in exploring philosophical debates. It was a quite unexpected meeting of minds.

Soon they were reading texts from great authors throughout the ages, as well as bringing along their own academic work to use as a basis for lectures, debates and discussions. It is believed that the first title they looked at was Karl Pearson's *The Grammar of Science*. Within a few weeks they added to their number Conrad Habicht, a mathematician and acquaintance of Einstein. Their meetings often lasted well into the night and, partly in recognition of the fact that he usually hosted them in his flat, Einstein was designated 'President of the Olympia Academy'. It was a tongue-in-cheek title at the time but few academies – however long established and renowned – could claim such an influence on twentieth-century thought.

The core of the Academy was these three, though others were allowed to attend now and again, including Habicht's brother, Paul, Michele Besso, Marcel Grossmann and Mileva Marić.

Meetings typically began with a meal, often most notable for its Spartan nature owing to the membership's combined lack of finances. On occasion, Einstein would break up the intellectual discussion with an impromptu violin recital. A remarkable bonhomie and companionship built up between the three but the Academy came to a natural conclusion when Habicht moved away in 1904 followed by Solovine the following year. But distance did not prevent them remaining lifelong friends and intellectual sparring partners.

Einstein never underestimated the influence of the group on the progress of his career. He sent letters to Habicht discussing some of his greatest discoveries and kept up a correspondence with Solovine – who would become his French-language publisher – all his life. In 1953 he wrote Solovine a commemoration of the Academy that shows just how warmly he remembered it:

In your short active life you have amused yourself about all in childish joy what was clear and clever. Your members have created you to laugh about your big, old and arrogant sisters [established academic academies]. How much they have hit bull's eye with this I have learnt through many years of thorough watching ... All three of us members have proved at least as lasting. Even if they are already a bit doddery, something of your happy and lively light shines on our lonely path of life ...

Do Your Homework!

'[Einstein was a] lazy dog.'

HERMANN MINKOWSKI,
ALBERT'S MATHEMATICS PROFESSOR

While it was apparent from an early age that Einstein had prodigious natural abilities in maths and science, it was not altogether clear that he would master the self-discipline required to see those talents blossom.

By 1895, the precocious teen Einstein had come far enough in his specialist subjects that he was producing his first serious scientific paper ('On the Investigation of the State of the Ether in a Magnetic Field'), and applied for a place in higher education two years early. Even so, he was found to be just shy of the required level in the general component of his entrance exam and was unsuccessful in his application. To his credit, he immediately took himself off for the further schooling he required and, as we have already seen, secured his place at Zurich Polytechnic. However, there is the inescapable conclusion that he had got a little ahead of himself, relying too much on his innate abilities. In this sense, he was no different to legions of bright-spark teens that preceded and have followed him. But a reluctance to put in the hard hours in areas that did not capture his imagination was a failing he indulged a while longer.

It is true that, having been found wanting in the general section of his polytechnic exam, he devoted himself to getting up to speed during his schooling in Aarau, Switzerland. It helped that he felt at one with the teaching ethos there, which was geared towards nurturing 'inner dignity' and encouraging each student to explore their individualism. The style of schooling owed much to the theories of the nineteenth-century Swiss educationalist, Johann Heinrich Pestalozzi. His philosophy called for learning through the head, hand and heart. He believed schooling should not be a process of a teacher 'telling' but that learning should instead engage the student's personality and involve activity, objects and visualization. Pupils were granted the freedom to pursue their own interests and draw their own conclusions. It was all a million miles from the strict regimen of his Prussian-influenced schooling in Germany and provided an atmosphere in which Einstein thrived.

However, once he started his studies at Zurich Polytechnic, he fell into some old habits as he kicked against the strictures of formal academe. It was becoming evident that Einstein was significantly stronger in physics than he was in maths, and he responded by focusing his attentions on his area of strength. In later life he would concede: 'It was not clear to me as a student that a more profound knowledge of the basic principles of physics was tied up with the most intricate mathematical methods.' The practical result was that he demonstrated a distinct lack of interest in his maths studies, so that his professor, Hermann Minkowski, remembered him as a 'lazy dog'.

Within his physics studies, too, he had clear preferences. He was, for instance, far more engrossed by the big questions of contemporary physics than he was in the historical aspects of the subject that provided the basis for much of the Zurich curriculum. He was also firmly anchored in the theoretical side of the discipline, rather than its applied fields. So much so that in 1899 one professor, Jean Pernet, failed him and pushed for the Polytechnic to write him an official letter of reprimand for his lax attitude to lab practice. A few months later, Einstein caused an explosion in one of Pernet's labs that resulted in a trip to the hospital to get the former's hand sewn up. The experience did little to encourage Einstein that his future lay in the practical side of physics. We can only wonder whether he may have influenced the incident, just as the reluctant cook sets out to burn the beans on toast so that he is not asked back into the kitchen again.

During his time studying in Zurich, he was quite the social animal and threw himself into the city's Bohemian scene. In the classic student manner, his eagerness to enjoy everything that life had to offer was reflected in a far from perfect attendance rate at lectures. He would come to rely on the good will and diligence of his friend Marcel Grossmann, who allowed Einstein to copy his notes and kept him on course in mathematics. It was another example of his sometimes lax attitude and reluctance to put in the hard yards that owed to his relatively lowly academic ranking compared to his fellow graduates.

His refusal to embrace formal academic discipline continued long after he had graduated as he struggled even to keep up with the literature relevant to his own particular areas of interest. For instance, in 1907 he blamed his failure to read everything written on relativity since his own landmark work in 1905 on the fact that 'the library is closed in my free time'!

It is perhaps meaningless to ask the question, 'What might Einstein have achieved if he'd paid closer attention to his geography and maths homework?' Nonetheless, it is not unfair to suggest that Einstein's early career might have met with fewer obstacles if he had knuckled down across all the academic disciplines and not just those in which he was naturally strong.

Challenge
Authority

'Long live impudence! It is my
guardian angel in this world.'

ALBERT EINSTEIN

His refusal to fully submit himself to the demands of the academic world was one reflection of the natural streak of rebelliousness that would prove so important in his theoretical work. Einstein, above all else, was an independent spirit with a natural adversity to bending to the will of others. He considered that the individual and society existed in a delicate balance in which the former must not be subsumed by the latter. In 1932 he would write: 'Without creative personalities able to think and judge independently, the upward development of society is as unthinkable as the development of the individual personality without the nourishing soil of the community.'

His anti-authoritarian roots were evident from early on. As much as he had loved his time at Aarau, he had hated his previous school, Munich's Luitpold Gymnasium, where he started aged eight, which prided itself on quasi-military discipline. Years later he would recall with barely disguised disgust how his fellow pupils would rush from their classrooms to watch military processions going past. 'When a person can take pleasure in marching in step to a piece of music,' he said, 'it is enough to make me despise him.' Einstein was intent on marching only to his own beat.

Having stayed behind in Munich to finish his schooling while the rest of his family moved to Italy, he found himself cast out from the Gymnasium at the end of 1894. It is uncertain whether this was a result of his being expelled – one teacher complained that his presence in class 'is disruptive and affects the other students' – or whether he withdrew himself. Either way, he swiftly set out to rejoin his family, whereas if he had remained in Germany for another year, he would have qualified for national service – an undertaking he would have detested. Such was his distaste for Germany by that stage that he soon gave up his citizenship, choosing instead to be stateless for several years.

His instinctive rejection of authority only increased as he entered early adulthood. In 1901, for instance, he would tell his friend Jost Winteler that 'a foolish faith in authority is the worst enemy of truth'. Around this time he had become interested in Paul Drude's research into electron transfer in materials but had criticisms of some of his findings. Precociously, he wrote to Drude to point out his mistakes, receiving in return a rather dismissive response. Drude, it should be remembered, was at the forefront of European science in this period. Einstein, though, was infuriated, vowing not to 'turn' to such people in future but 'instead attack them in the journals, as they deserve'. The whole experience left him to conclude that: 'It is no wonder that little by little one becomes a misanthrope.'

Einstein's heroes were those who used their intellect to challenge the status quo. His inherent distrust of accepting what one is presented with was part of the reason that he so admired Galileo, who he considered had waged a 'passionate fight against any kind of dogma based on authority'. It was why Einstein was prepared to question literally everything – including the accepted fundamental principles of our cosmos. The pay-off was that he regularly found himself in conflict with institutions of governance, with professional colleagues and sometimes with dangerous enemies. Nonetheless, there is the strong suspicion that he was never more alive than when locked in such struggle.

In advice to the New York State Education Department in the 1950s, Einstein argued that history should be taught through the wide discussion of 'personalities who benefited mankind through independence of character and judgement'. In Einstein's view, such figures are paragons because, as he explained in 1952, 'only the individual can produce the new ideas'.

… But Don't Make Unnecessary Enemies

'It is difficult to make him your enemy,
but once he has cast you out of his heart,
you are done for as far as he is concerned.'

JANOS PLESCH (EINSTEIN'S DOCTOR)

E instein's iconoclasm and fearless refusal to accept things as they are was doubtless key to his work in theoretical physics. The theory of relativity could only have been countenanced by someone unafraid to overthrow long-held principles. He was also remarkably courageous in taking on opponents seemingly far more powerful than himself – from the Nazis to the McCarthyites of Cold War America.

This desire to challenge was at its most potent after Einstein became established as a global figure, intellectual icon and moral authority. However, there were times in his life when his refusal to bow to others made him enemies without good reason and came at the greatest cost to himself. This is most evident in the period he spent as a student at Zurich Polytechnic and the years immediately afterwards.

Einstein, the loner child with a mind full of ideas and images that few others could relate to, was always likely to seem a little distant. Being a Jew in an era of rising anti-Semitism only increased his sense of being an outsider. By the time he was a young man he had a reputation for aloofness. As he acknowledged in one of his impassioned letters to Mileva Marić, he knew that he could be moody, not to mention mischievous and sometimes even roguish.

His brashness infuriated senior figures at the Polytechnic, among them his main physics professor, Heinrich Weber. Einstein made little secret that he did not enjoy the syllabus Weber offered, while alienating other members of the faculty who now considered him more a nuisance than a nascent genius. By the time he graduated, many of the staff had him marked down as a troublemaker, seriously impacting his chances of getting a job at his *alma mater*.

In truth, he did little to help himself in this. For instance, he applied for a post under his former maths professor, Adolf Hurwitz, despite having skipped a large number of his seminars. When he made his application, Einstein rather weakly asserted that he had, however, gone to most of Hurwitz's lectures and pleaded for a job on the grounds that his bid for Swiss citizenship depended upon it. It was hardly a winning approach and he was the only one of his undergraduate intake not to secure a position at the Polytechnic. Iconoclasm is one thing but a self-defeating refusal to play the game is quite another. At this stage of his life, Einstein seemed unable to distinguish between the two.

And so the disappointing start to his academic career continued. His first published paper in 1901 (on capillary effect) failed to wow the world and was later described by Einstein himself as 'worthless'. He fired off letters to disparate corners of Europe in search of academic postings to no avail. By Easter of 1901, his parents were beckoning him to join them in Milan until he could find a job. Einstein was convinced that his chances were being hampered by unfavourable references from Heinrich Weber. But if you want a good reference, someone might have warned him, don't upset your referee. More darkly, he also suspected that he suffered as the result of anti-Semitic feeling, particularly from institutions in his native Germany.

It was his old friend Marcel Grossmann who came to the rescue when he notified Einstein of an upcoming vacancy in the Bern patent office. Einstein finally took up a position there in 1902 but it was hardly the springboard to greatness that he might have hoped for – and, in part, it was his reckless accumulation of opponents (and casual disregard for potential allies) that had landed him there.

THE (RELATIVE) STRUGGLE FOR A PROFESSORSHIP

Beginning as a Technical Expert (Class 3), Einstein spent seven years at the patent office, often working six long days a week. He did not leave his job until 1909 – four years after he had published his special theory. If it is easy enough to understand how his academic career had stalled back in 1900, it is astonishing to contemplate that no academic institution had the foresight to snap him up after such an outpouring of scientific thought.

It has been argued by some that Einstein's richly creative output in this period was partly thanks to his role at the patent office. Inspecting innumerable practical applications no doubt helped hone his analytical skills. He also had plenty of time sitting at a desk and carrying out relatively undemanding tasks, which allowed his creative imagination to get to work. He himself came to believe that he had probably benefited from being outside the academic machine, which would have demanded a conveyor belt of research papers from him. The temptation, he felt, would have been to churn out mundane work. The patent office allowed him to focus on only the extraordinary.

However, post-1905, he still longed to secure a decently paid academic role that would give him greater room to pursue his private studies. Yet, his reluctance to do what was expected of him was still costing him. In 1907 he applied for a junior position at the University of Bern but failed to produce for them an unpublished paper as required. The following year he was even turned down for a post teaching maths in a Zurich school, despite including his various papers in his application. In fact, he was not even shortlisted!

At last, in February 1908, he was awarded his

first academic position as a *Privatdozent* (a junior academic) at the University of Bern. Alas, the money was so bad that he was compelled to keep up his patent office job even as he started to lecture. The prospect of a posting that would allow him more room for his private studies seemed as distant as ever. It was not until the following year that he took up his first professorship, at the University of Zurich, the rival institution to his undergraduate *alma mater*.

By most accounts, his lectures were not particularly captivating considering the mass of knowledge he had at his disposal. He was often unprepared and performed on the hoof. Teaching did not seem to be in his blood. That was a shame, considering that in his later life he had much of interest to say about the art of teaching. For instance, in 1934 he contributed a quotation for the US National Council of Supervisors of Elementary Science:

> The most valuable thing a teacher can impart to children is not knowledge and understanding per se but a *longing* for knowledge and understanding, and an appreciation for intellectual values, whether they be artistic, scientific, or moral.

It was a sentiment he echoed in a speech two years later: 'The aim must be the training of independently acting and thinking individuals who, however, see in the service to the community their highest life achievement.'

But for all his faults as a lecturer, he clearly developed considerable attributes as a communicator for those with the intellect and the desire to engage. In a letter aimed at bringing Einstein back to Zurich from his posting in Prague in 1911, Heinrich Zangger wrote:

He is not a good teacher for mentally lazy gentlemen who merely want to fill up a notebook and then learn it by heart for an exam; he is not a smooth talker. But anyone who wants to learn how to construct physical ideas, carefully examine all premises, take note of the pitfalls and problems, review the reliability of his reflections, will find Einstein a first-rate teacher.

That Einstein's passage through academe was so troubled even after he had produced the work that would win him a Nobel Prize and make him a household name must rank among the great mysteries of the twentieth century. That said, it is clear that he was sometimes his own worst enemy.

Make Hay While the Sun Shines

'Anything truly novel is invented
only during one's youth.'

ALBERT EINSTEIN

Despite the disappointing start to his academic career, Einstein did not let it get in the way of what really mattered: wrestling with the big questions of science. Ignored by Europe's great institutions of learning, he dutifully clocked in and out of the Bern Patent Office and used every available spare minute to explore his extraordinary ideas. When inspiration struck, he proved that he did not need the respect or support of any science faculty to make the next great leap in creative thinking.

That was fortunate, because Einstein would become convinced that the most innovative leaps forward are made almost exclusively by the young. 1905, the year he turned twenty-six years of age, is generally regarded as his *annus mirabilis*, his miracle year. Already by 1906 he was starting to worry that he would soon reach the 'age of stagnation and sterility when one laments the revolutionary spirit of the young'. Of course, there was still much to come from Einstein, including the general theory of relativity and a long search for a unified field theory. But it is equally true that his most remarkable work was completed by the time he was forty.

Make Hay While the Sun Shines

As he became an ever bigger global figure and used a proportion of his time to promote his political and humanitarian interests, he no longer found himself at the cusp of innovation. As his areas of special interest became flooded with new research and literature, much of it inspired by his own work, he found himself unable to keep up with the reading of it all. He also lost some of that intuitive feel for where the next great innovations might come from, as evidenced by his often pained pursuit of a unified field theory. The impact of age on the power of his mind deeply troubled him, and he spoke in terms of the crippling of the intellect. Reaching his half-century was particularly hard and he would write of the 'increasing difficulty of adapting to new thoughts which always confront the man past fifty'.

It may have been a disappointment for Einstein that his greatest triumphs came early, as it is natural to desire personal progression. But for those who came afterwards, what mattered most are the achievements themselves rather than when they occurred in his life. For us, we need only be grateful that he had the wherewithal in relative youth to bring his inspirations to fruition.

So just what was it that made 1905 such an *annus mirabilis*? The answer, in short, is four scientific papers, each of which contributed to a rewriting of the rules of science. At the start of the twentieth century, mankind inhabited a Newtonian universe that had held sway for over two centuries. Over that time, it had provided humanity with a degree of certainty. Everything could be explained by cause and effect. Objects moved and behaved in specific ways because of particular forces acting upon them. In Einstein's words: 'In the beginning (if there was such a thing), God created Newton's laws of motion together with the necessary masses and forces.'

Of course, science had not stood still since Newton's death in 1727. For instance, Michael Faraday's work in the mid-nineteenth century on electrical and magnetic fields provided a basis for James Clerk Maxwell's investigations into electromagnetic waves. The existence of the electromagnetic field fascinated Einstein, who called it 'the most important invention since Newton's time'. But it was Einstein himself who had the vision and intellectual courage to make the next great leaps.

The bulk of the work on his landmark 1905 papers was done during an outpouring of inspiration between March and June. He wrote to his Olympia Academy co-founder, Conrad Habicht, breaking the 'solemn air of silence' between them with 'some inconsequential babble'. He then briefly outlined his four earth-shattering papers.

THE 1905 PAPERS

The first paper, which Einstein described as 'very revolutionary', dealt with radiation and the energy properties of light. It would prove to be crucial to the development of quantum theory. Building on the work of Maxwell, Gustav Kirchhoff and Max Planck, he concluded that light existed in minuscule packets that we now refer to as photons. This revelation allowed quantum mechanics to ultimately conclude that light exists in a strange duality as both wave *and* particle.

Einstein was intrinsically nervous of the quantum world Planck's work suggested, stating that it was 'as if the ground had been pulled out from under us, with no firm foundation to be seen anywhere'. Yet his first paper of 1905 took the abstract theory of Planck and gave it physical reality. This was truly mind-bending stuff and even Einstein seemed overwhelmed by his own ideas. He described the paper as a 'heuristic point of view' – in other words, a hypothesis aimed at pointing the way towards a solution, but not a proven thesis. It included the following passage:

According to the assumption to be considered here, when a light ray is propagated from a point, the energy is not continuously distributed over an increasing space but consists of a finite number of energy quanta which are localized at points in space and which can be produced and absorbed only as complete units.

This was, according to his biographer Walter Isaacson, 'the most revolutionary sentence that Einstein ever wrote'. Even having made his astonishing breakthrough, some of the precise detail of its physical reality remained elusive. Shortly before he died, Einstein freely admitted that after fifty years of going over the issue, he was no nearer to understanding just what light quanta are.

The second paper, on the 'determination of the true size of atoms', would earn him his better-late-than-never doctorate. However, designed for a specific academic purpose, it was, in comparison with the other papers in the series, relatively low key. The third paper, meanwhile, was an investigation of Brownian motion using statistical analysis that confirmed the actual existence of atoms and molecules. Hitherto, there had been many who had reasoned their existence but there was little in the way of observable evidence.

Then came the fourth paper, outlining the special theory of relativity. He had described it to Habicht as 'only a rough draft at this point', which looked into the electrodynamics of moving bodies and 'employs a modification of the theory of space and time'. It is difficult to imagine a cooler, more composed way to announce that you were about to fundamentally change mankind's understanding of the universe.

It was as he worked on this paper that some of the thought experiments we have previously mentioned came into their own. Riding alongside a light beam in his imagination, Einstein had realized that if he could keep up with the beam, surely it would appear to be stationary – just as if you were to peer through a train window at another train going in the same direction and at the same speed as you, it would not appear to be moving. Yet Maxwell's electromagnetic theories did not allow for this, so Einstein knew there must be an alternative explanation. Similarly, by studying the lightning-struck train he recognized that the same event could look different to alternate subjects.

Einstein was by no means the first scientist to consider the questions raised in the special theory. Others had got very close to reaching several of his conclusions. But what Einstein brought to relativity was a willingness to dispense with notions that were once considered irrefutable truths. So, for instance, he developed the work of Henri Poincaré, who in the 1880s had questioned the existence of a quasi-mystical ether through which light was thought to travel. He expanded on the work of the Dutch physicist Heinrich Lorentz, who had devised complex mathematics to explain the results of the famous 1887 Michelson–Morley experiment into the speed of light. But it was Einstein who then made the truly bold leaps of the imagination that others were unable to make.

So came about the special theory of relativity, in which Einstein asserted that the laws of physics are the same for all observers moving at a constant velocity relative to each other, and that the speed of light in a vacuum is constant. All of which meant that where the Newtonian world decreed that space and time were absolute, Einstein showed that they were not. For many, this latter conclusion was the only headline: another of life's 'certainties' had been dismantled. In the first decade of the twentieth century, the world was still struggling with the implications of Darwin's teachings of a few decades before and was fumbling its way into the modern age against a backdrop of radical cultural innovations and fundamental challenges to social and moral conventions. Now here was a scientist saying that not even the way your clock ticked or the space it inhabited on your mantelpiece were quite as they seemed.

Yet Einstein's reputation as an overturner of 'truths' depends, at least to a degree, on how you look at things. It's all relative, you might say. Yes, he was the author of the theory of relativity, and the very word 'relativity' suggests doubt and uncertainty. However, it was initially his intention to call it the theory of 'invariance', for he was also describing the immutability of fundamental physical laws. Had he succeeded in establishing this naming convention, his own name would have been intrinsically entwined with a word that suggests not doubt but certainty. That would have been a far more accurate reflection of Einstein, whose whole scientific *raison d'être* was to find *rules* and *laws* to explain why our world and the universe is as it is. Adding to the early twentieth-century milieu of upheaval was of little interest to him. All of which goes to show that most fundamental truth of all: branding is everything.

Never one to stand still, Einstein even had time for a fifth paper, which emerged directly out of the special theory. Entitled 'Does the Inertia of a Body depend on Its Energy Content?', it was published in *Annalen der Physik* in September 1905 and was just three pages long. Its conclusions, though, were startling. Einstein had found that a body's mass is a proportional measure of its energy content. In other words, mass and energy are different presentations of the same thing. The insight would come to be illustrated with the most famous equation in history: $E = mc^2$ (energy = mass multiplied by the speed of light squared). For the layman, this meant that something very small could contain an awful lot of energy. Though Einstein had no idea how it would play out, he had just ushered in the Nuclear Age.

In one final curious aside to the story, the famous equation did not actually appear in Einstein's 1905 paper. In fact, he wrote, 'If a body emits the energy L in the form of radiation, its mass decreases by L/V^2.' L was the symbol he used for energy for several more years to come and V was his shorthand for the velocity of light. So if the equation had appeared at all in the format with which we are now familiar, it would actually have read: $L = mV^2$.

If Einstein's 1905 output had been stretched out over a career spanning several decades, it would have been extraordinary. That he had this disparate array of subjects going through his mind in such a condensed period of time and that he was able to bring such insight into the problems they threw up is almost beyond comprehension.

How to Read
Like Einstein

'Don't read any newspapers, find a few like-minded people and read the wonderful writers of the past, Kant, Goethe, Lessing, and the classics of other countries …'

ALBERT EINSTEIN, 1933

Einstein's attitude to reading varied over his lifetime. In some periods, he was a voracious reader – the Olympia Academy, for instance, greedily consumed books of many different genres. Referring specifically to the literary art form in 1920, he said: 'Personally, I experience the greatest degree of pleasure in having contact with works of art. They furnish me with happy feelings of an intensity that I cannot derive from other sources.'

However, there were times when he felt that too much energy spent reading was a waste. He told the interviewer G. S. Viereck in 1929:

Reading, after a certain age, diverts the mind too much from its creative pursuits. Any man who reads too much and uses his own brain too little falls into lazy habits of thinking, just as the man who spends too much time in the theatre is tempted to be content with living vicariously instead of living his own life.

However, it is worth remembering that these words were spoken at a time when Einstein was increasingly interested in political causes, while also going through one of his less immediately productive periods as a scientist. With this in mind, it is understandable that he regarded reading as a distraction from what he really wanted to be doing. But looking at his life as a whole, it is clear that he was an avid and broad reader.

In terms of 'great' literature, his interests spread from the ancients to the moderns. Sophocles' *Antigone* was a particular favourite among the works of the Classical Greeks. Given some of its themes – the battle between the individual and the state, ruminations on natural law – it should not be a surprise that it captivated him so.

He also fell in love with Miguel de Cervantes' seventeenth-century classic, *Don Quixote*, which appealed to both his sense of the comic and the tragic. As he grew older and found himself at odds with many of science's prevailing trends, he may also have seen echoes of himself in Don Quixote tilting at windmills.

Among the authors of his homeland, he held none in higher esteem than Johann Wolfgang von Goethe and Gotthold Lessing. Goethe was a true literary superstar of the late-eighteenth and early-nineteenth centuries. A poet, dramatist, novelist, memoirist, critic and scientific writer, he was at the forefront of the Romantic *Sturm und Drang* movement and his influence on German letters is felt to this day. Einstein began studying him in his teens and accumulated more of his works (a total of fifty-two volumes) than any other writer's.

Lessing, meanwhile, was an eighteenth-century German poet, philosopher, critic and dramatist of the Enlightenment. His most famous works include *Miss Sara Sampson*, *Minna von Barnhelm*, *Emilia Galotti* and *Nathan the Wise*. Lessing espoused freedom of thought and promoted the power of reason, while eschewing blind faith in religious doctrine. Einstein once noted: 'It is open to every man to choose the direction of his striving; and also every man may draw comfort from Lessing's fine saying, that the search for truth is more precious than its possession.' The scientist was also an admirer of the nineteenth century radical German-Jewish Romantic poet and essayist, Heinrich Heine. Heine's radical politics ultimately forced him into exile and he is perhaps most famous today for his words later engraved at the sight of the Nazi book burnings in Berlin: 'That was but a prelude; where they burn books, they will ultimately burn people also.'

Of authors working in his own lifetime, Einstein felt a natural affinity with the great Russian writers, Leo Tolstoy and Fyodor Dostoyevsky (the latter of whom died shortly before Einstein's second birthday). In a 1935 interview, he described Tolstoy as 'in many ways the foremost prophet of our time ... There is no one today with Tolstoy's deep insight and moral force.' Meanwhile, he described Dostoyevsky's last novel, *The Brothers Karamazov* – a study of faith and doubt – to his friend

Paul Ehrenfest in 1920 as 'the most wonderful book I have ever put my hands on'.

Einstein also had notable friendships with two Nobel Literature laureates: Rabindranath Tagore and George Bernard Shaw. It was with Shaw that he had the greater meeting of minds, the pair having been introduced at a private dinner in 1921. Shaw admired the scientist for the way he had overthrown what he saw as a complacent faith in scientific infallibility. He delivered a speech in 1931 in which he identified Einstein as one of eight 'makers of universes' over the previous 2,500 years (the rest of the esteemed gang being Pythagoras, Ptolemy, Kepler, Copernicus, Aristotle, Galileo and Newton). On the other hand, Einstein believed Shaw to be 'one of the world's greatest figures', whose plays 'remind me of Mozart'.

Einstein also had a good grounding in philosophical works. He read Immanuel Kant (1724-1804), for instance – in particular the 1781 *Critique of Pure Reason* and 1783's *Prolegomena*. These explore fundamental questions of what we know and how we know it, looking at how our knowledge is conditioned by our minds and senses, as well as investigating the processes of generating knowledge from observation and logic.

Also important was David Hume's *A Treatise of Human Nature*, (1739-40), in which he argued that knowledge could only be proven through observation by the senses, thus laying the path for positivism. It was a work that Einstein studied, in his own words, 'avidly and with admiration' shortly before formulating his theory of relativity. As a young man, he also read John Stuart Mill's *System of Logic* (1843), which considered how logic works, including discussions of inductive reasoning and an analysis of causation, a clear influence on Einstein's own methods. Baruch Spinoza was another significant influence, particularly in regard to Einstein's attitude towards religion – a subject we will look at in due course.

THE LITERATURE OF SCIENCE

At university Einstein would often skip classes so that he could use the time to read up on those he called the 'masters of theoretical physics'. It would, of course, be impossible to list all of the writers who influenced him over his lifetime. However, here is a short selection of the authors and works that we know he read in the period leading up to his *annus mirabilis* of 1905:

⊙ Aaron Bernstein (1812–1884). A German Jew whose *The People's Natural Science Books* was read voraciously by the young Einstein. One story depicting electricity transference along a telegraph wire is widely held to have inspired Einstein's light beam thought experiment.

⊙ Ludwig Boltzmann (1844–1906). Responsible for advances in electromagnetism and thermodynamics, he is most famed for his development of statistical mechanics that built on the work of James Clerk Maxwell. Statistical mechanics describes physical phenomena by looking statistically at the behaviour of large numbers of atoms and molecules. Prone to depression, Boltzmann committed suicide in 1906.

⊙ Paul Drude (1863–1906). Drude made his name by combining his specialism, optics, with James Clerk Maxwell's theories of electromagnetism. In 1900 he published his *Theory of Optics*, which integrated the study of electricity and optics in an entirely new way. He was also responsible for the Drude model, which deals with the transport of electrons within materials (especially metals). Like Boltzmann, he too committed suicide in 1906 while at the peak of his career.

⊙ Pierre Duhem (1861–1916). Duhem carried out significant work in the fields of elasticity, hydrodynamics and thermodynamics. But perhaps more important for Einstein were his writings on the philosophy of science, and in particular the relationship between theory and experiment.

⊙ Euclid (*fl.* third century BC). A Greek mathematician whose *Elements* laid out the basic rules of geometry as we know them today, as well as covering other aspects of mathematics. Einstein was presented with a copy of the work when he was twelve and called it the 'holy geometry book'.

- ⊙ Michael Faraday (1791–1867). An English inventor and pioneer of electromagnetism and electrochemistry. Einstein kept a picture of him on his wall, alongside ones of Newton and Maxwell. Notable works include two volumes of *Experimental Researches in Electricity*, *Experimental Researches in Chemistry and Physics* and *On the Various Forces in Nature*.

- ⊙ August Föppl (1854–1924). A professor at the Technical University of Munich whose 1894 *Introduction to Maxwell's Theory of Electricity* was read by Einstein and influenced his ideas regarding relativity.

- ⊙ Galileo Galilei (1564–1642). An Italian scientific revolutionary and one of Einstein's heroes. Einstein was familiar with his life's works, which included *On Motion* (1590), *Mechanics* (*c.* 1600) and *Discourse on Floating Bodies* (1612).

- ⊙ Hermann von Helmholtz (1821–1894). A physicist and scientific philosopher who carried out notable work in areas including non-Euclidian geometry, field theory and energy conservation. His writings also include discussion of the relationship between scientific theory and experimentation. Key works include

On the Conservation of Force (1847) and his 1885 collection of *Popular Lectures on Scientific Subjects*.

- ⊙ Heinrich Hertz (1857–1894). Hertz, a German who lent his name to the international unit of frequency and carried out experiments that proved Maxwell's electromagnetic theory. His significant achievements came in a life cut short by illness after just thirty-six years. His papers were collected in three volumes: *Electric Waves* (1893), *Miscellaneous Papers* (1896) and *Principles of Mechanics* (1899).

- ⊙ Gustav Kirchhoff (1824–1887). A German physicist key to establishing the theory of spectrum analysis. He also devised several electrical laws and found that current flows through a conductor at the speed of light. His collection *Lectures on Mathematical Physics* held particular resonance for Einstein.

- ⊙ Hendrik Lorentz (1853–1928). Dutch physicist and joint recipient of the 1902 Nobel Prize for his research into the influence of magnetism upon radiation phenomena. His 1895 work *Attempt at a Theory of Electrical and Optical Phenomena in Moving Bodies* was pivotal in Einstein's formulation of the special theory. The two men subsequently became close friends and colleagues, with Lorentz assisting Einstein in the mathematics required for the general theory.

⊙ Ernst Mach (1838–1916). An Austrian physicist and philosopher whose published works include *Mechanics and Its Development* (1883) and *The Analysis of Sensations* (1897). In common with Einstein, he was a free thinker and political idealist. His critique of Newtonian absolute time and space was highly influential on the young Einstein.

⊙ James Clerk Maxwell (1831–1879). A Scottish mathematical physicist, his most famous work was in the field of electromagnetic radiation. Papers such as 'A Dynamical Theory of the Electromagnetic Field' (1864) and 'On a Method of Making a Direct Comparison of Electrostatic with Electromagnetic Force; with a Note on the Electromagnetic Theory of Light' (1865) were hugely influential on Einstein and informed his development of the theory of relativity. Einstein would note: 'The work of James Clerk Maxwell changed the world forever.' High praise indeed.

⊙ Isaac Newton (1642–1727). Before Einstein, there was Newton. His 1687 *Philosophiæ Naturalis Principia Mathematica* (*Mathematical Principles of Natural Philosophy*) set out his laws of motion and theory of gravity that underpinned science for the best part of the next two and a half centuries.

⊙ Karl Pearson (1857–1936). An English mathematician who helped establish the modern discipline of statistics. His 1892 work, *The Grammar of Science*, was reputedly the first text read and considered by the Olympia Academy. It introduced a number of the scientific themes that would occupy Einstein during his career.

⊙ Max Planck (1858–1947). A German theoretical physicist whose career significantly overlapped with Einstein's. A supporter of Einstein's work, Planck became a close colleague although they viewed quantum mechanics very differently. Einstein's special theory developed certain ideas of Planck's outlined in papers including 'The Principle of the Conservation of Energy' (1887) and 'On the Theory of the Energy Distribution Law of the Normal Spectrum' (1900).

⊙ Henri Poincaré (1854–1912). A French polymath whom many believe deserves greater credit for presaging several elements of the special theory. Einstein was a significant admirer of Poincaré's 1902 work, *Science and Hypothesis*, a philosophical treatise on the nature of science and the formulation of theory.

Immerse Yourself

'Strenuous intellectual work and looking at God's nature are the reconciling, fortifying yet relentlessly strict angels that shall lead me through all of life's troubles.'

ALBERT EINSTEIN, 1897

Einstein's intellectual brilliance was allied to a formidable work ethic that found him scribbling equations in an old notepad right up until a few hours before his death. It was Thomas Edison who said that genius is one per cent inspiration and ninety-nine per cent perspiration, and, although there is room for bargaining on the exact proportions, this basic rule applied to Einstein.

His attitude to self-sacrifice for his work is summed up by an observation he made in 1927: 'If there is no price to be paid, it is also not of value.' In 1954 he developed the point when telling his son, Hans Albert, that they shared a key trait: 'the ability to rise above mere existence by sacrificing one's self through the years for an impersonal goal'. But in truth, as we shall see, his dedication to his work was not entirely selfless and sometimes came at the expense of others. He could certainly appear aloof and off-hand to the casual observer and from childhood found himself with a reputation for self-absorption.

He undoubtedly saw work as a way to avoid confronting uncomfortable personal situations. In 1913, for instance, against the backdrop of his failing marriage, he said: 'The love of science thrives under these circumstances for it lifts me impersonally from the vale of tears into peaceful spheres.' It is intriguing to think that the formulation of the general theory of relativity offered him some form of emotional release.

But the work also took its toll. He was not one to slip off to his office and put his feet up on the desk until a flash of inspiration struck. His working environment was simple but chaotic, his desk (and any other available surface) commonly littered with piles of papers. He always had to hand a waste paper basket, into which he would agonizingly 'throw away all my mistakes'. He had a habit of pacing as he tried to untangle some teasing equation, and regularly neglected to feed and water himself properly – an attitude that came to seriously affect his health.

Even at university, when it is tempting to see him as a Bohemian figure doing pretty much what he wanted, he was already pushing himself hard. For the duration of his career, the occasional glories broke up repeated cycles of exhaustion and disappointment. Yet it was his choice to live this way, such was the satisfaction that he gained from scaling those peaks (and perhaps because he felt duty bound to scale them, too). Happiness for Einstein seems to have been found less in a contented personal life or the accumulation of material wealth (though he did not underestimate either) than in intellectual achievement. 'If you want to live a happy life,' he told his one-time assistant Ernst Straus, 'tie it to a goal, not to people or objects.'

Although he had a complex relationship with the cult of celebrity that was thrust upon him from the late 1910s onwards, he found the way it impinged on his theoretical work infuriating. According to his colleague and biographer, Banesh Hoffmann, Einstein had grown up wanting nothing more than to be allowed to sit in some quiet corner carrying out his work away from the public gaze. 'And now see what has become of me!' he is said to have exclaimed. It is a theme he returned to time and again. In London in 1933 he spoke of how 'the monotony of a quiet life' stimulates thinking and on another occasion he asserted that the ideal occupation for the theoretical scientist was as a lighthouse keeper. Science for Einstein was clearly a lonely and unglamorous business that required total concentration.

But for all that, the joy to be found in the work made it all worthwhile. When he was well into his fifties, he would tell Hans Albert that 'work is the only thing that gives substance to life'.

Don't Neglect Those Closest to You

'I have never belonged wholeheartedly to country or state, to my circle of friends, or even to my own family. These ties have always been accompanied by a vague aloofness …'

ALBERT EINSTEIN, 1932

For better or worse, then, Einstein devoted himself body and soul to his work for the large part of his life. Better, it goes without saying, for humanity as a whole, but worse for those closest to him.

It would be quite wrong to regard Einstein as a loner. He was close to his family as a child, had two wives, several children, numerous affairs and a large circle of friends and associates. While some struggled to know quite what to make of him, many of them spoke of him in glowing terms and he commanded great loyalty. And yet it was one of Einstein's good friends and regular quantum sparring partners who perhaps summed it up best: 'For all his kindness, sociability and love of humanity,' said Max Born, 'he was nevertheless totally detached from his environment and the human beings in it.'

Perhaps this was a little over-stated, but not excessively so. The evidence of his life suggests that Einstein was terrific at being a decent friend but struggled to maintain sound relations as the other party's emotional demands upon him increased. Thus it was possible for Einstein to build an admirably close relationship with his fellow Nobel Prize-winning physicist Hendrik Lorentz but to allow the bonds with successive wives and his children to fray.

Of Lorentz he would say that he admired him 'like no other; I might say, I love him'. Indeed, when Einstein was old, he would reflect on the man who had acted as his surrogate father figure for several years, saying 'he meant more to me personally than anybody else I have met in my lifetime'. Einstein's younger son, Eduard, had a far more complicated relationship with his own father, a situation not helped by serious mental ill-health. He once said:'It's at times difficult to have such an important father, because one feels so unimportant.' It is hardly a resounding endorsement of Einstein's parenting skills.

So what was the problem? It is fair to say that Einstein's mind lent itself more to scientific analysis than to empathy. He had an unfortunate penchant for trampling on the feelings of others, evident from early on in his life. In 1895, for example, as he lodged with the Winteler family in Aarau, the sixteen-year-old Albert fell for the family's eighteen-year-old daughter, Marie. By the time he moved to Zurich to continue his studies the following year, he found the strength of his ardour fading (though not enough to prompt him to stop sending his laundry to her). Marie, though, was still in love with him, perhaps even more so. In the end, he extricated himself from the relationship by first stopping his correspondence with her and then refusing to visit. It was a blunt approach and almost certainly crueller than was needed, leaving the distraught girl in a bout of depression.

Einstein himself came to realize that he was averse to intense emotional attachments. In 1917 he would tell his friend Heinrich Zangger (who also mediated in the ongoing dispute between Albert and his first wife, Mileva): 'I have come to know the mutability of all human relationships and have learned to insulate myself against both heat and cold so that a temperature balance is fairly well assured.' That sounds less like a case of temperature balance than cold-bloodedness. By then he was living separately from Mileva and felt that he would never again surrender the opportunity to live alone 'which has manifested itself as an indescribable blessing'.

There was also the issue of his commitment to his work, which we have already seen left little room for anything else. In a letter written to his mother in 1897 he had spoken of how 'strenuous intellectual work and looking at God's nature' would be the 'strict angels that shall lead me through all of life's troubles'. He then went on to concede that 'in many a lucid moment I appear to myself as an ostrich who buries his head in the desert sand so as not to perceive the danger'. Work, then, already offered a way to dodge emotional attachment. On another occasion, he wrote: 'I resemble a farsighted man who is charmed by the vast horizon and whom the foreground bothers only when an opaque object prevents him from taking in the long view.' It seems he was remarkably aware of how he was hiding from his personal life in his passion for physics.

It was a subject he touched upon again in an address

he gave for Max Planck's sixtieth birthday in 1918. 'One of the strongest motives that leads men to art and science is escape from everyday life with its painful crudity and hopeless dreariness.' He continued, 'Such men make this cosmos and its construction the pivot of their emotional life, in order to find the peace and security which they cannot find in the narrow whirlpool of personal experience.'

Others had their own take on his emotional deficiencies. Leopold Infeld said, 'I do not know anyone as lonely and detached as Einstein … His heart never bleeds, and he moves through life with mild enjoyment and emotional indifference. His extreme kindness and decency are thoroughly impersonal and seem to come from another planet.'

Towards the end of his life, both his secretary, Helen Dukas, his beloved sister Maja and his stepdaughter Margot were effectively living with him, the latter two seemingly rather keener to spend their time in his company than with their own husbands. Clearly, then, he was by no means impossible to co-habit with and perhaps had even mellowed somewhat by then. Equally, though, these were relationships in which not too much was expected of him. He was not, for instance, required to provide an emotional crutch as might be expected by a spouse.

In his 1949 essay, 'Why Socialism?', Einstein stated: 'Man is, at one and the same time, a solitary being and a social being.' That was certainly true in his case.

A FLAWED HUSBAND

'Marriage is but slavery made to appear civilized.'

ALBERT EINSTEIN AS QUOTED BY
KONRAD WACHSMANN

Part 1: Mileva Marić

Einstein was quite simply unsuited to the institution of marriage, but that did not stop him giving it two goes. Neither wife had an easy time of it, although it was his first wife who got the worse deal. His treatment of both reflects not only the emotional disconnects that could afflict him but also points to a man who – even though viewed by the outside world as a person of deep humanity – could be ruthless to those of whom he should have been most protective.

Having rather callously dispensed with the affections of Marie Winteler, he would next lose his heart to a fellow student at Zurich Polytechnic, a girl called Mileva Marić who hailed from what is now Serbia.

Born a few years before Einstein, in 1875, Mileva was a bright spark. The daughter of a successful former peasant and soldier, she excelled at the sciences and in 1894 graduated from the traditionally all-male Zagreb Royal Classical High School with the highest marks in the year. In

Zurich she was the only female studying physics among that year's student intake.

She and Einstein immediately hit it off, although to many onlookers it seemed a somewhat unlikely alliance. She had a history of poor health that included tuberculosis and a hip complaint that caused her to walk with a pronounced limp – an unfortunate set of circumstances reflected in an often gloomy disposition. Einstein, meanwhile, was handsome and virtually had his pick of the local women. But theirs was a meeting of minds, a slow-burning love affair with its roots in mutual intellectual admiration.

Things really ignited between them after Mileva returned from a term's study at the University of Heidelberg. After an initial period of cautious flirtation, they were soon immersed in an intense affair marked by fervent ups as well as regular downs. It is documented in their impassioned correspondence that veers one moment from teenager-like declarations of love (especially from Einstein: '... without you my life is not life') to almost comic triviality ('We understand each other's dark souls so well, and also drinking coffee and eating sausages, etc.'). Crucially, for Einstein at least, the relationship offered the opportunity to progress his scientific endeavours rather than presenting an obstacle. Mileva may not have been the 'looker' that some of his friends thought would be more suited to him, but she was a female who could keep decent pace with his own intellectualism. In one letter, for instance, he spoke of looking forward to an imminent reunion in some vivid detail before finishing with the memorable line: 'And then we'll start on Helmholtz's electromagnetic theory of light.'

Mileva had high hopes for an academic career of her own, but her ambitions started to derail when she failed her final exams in 1900 and again in 1901. By the time she sat them for a second time, she was already pregnant with Einstein's child, a daughter born back in Novi Sad in Mileva's homeland in early 1902. Einstein vowed to look after them all. 'My scientific goals and my personal vanity,' he assured her, 'will not prevent me from accepting even the most subordinate position.' He would not, though, agree to marry her, and there were nascent strains in the relationship.

Their daughter was named Lieserl, but what happened to her is an enduring mystery. Einstein's attitude to fatherhood at this stage was decidedly ambiguous. Before Lieserl's birth, and while he and Mileva were living in different countries, he wrote of his daughter: 'I love her so much and don't even know her yet!' But he did not rush off to Serbia after the birth and there is no evidence to suggest any of his friends or family knew of the child. He knew his parents would not approve, as they held Mileva in low opinion. (Ironically, Einstein would be even more critical of his son Hans Albert's choice of an older partner decades later.) When Mileva rejoined Einstein in Switzerland, she was alone, having left Lieserl back at home. There is speculation that the child died from scarlet fever in 1903, although it is possible that she was given up for adoption. Einstein certainly never made reference to his lost daughter at any point afterwards, which suggests this was a particularly sad, and possibly dark, episode for all involved.

Despite their already fractious relationship, Einstein and Mileva married at last in early 1903. The ceremony was witnessed by members of the Olympia Academy but notably none of Einstein's family were present. In spite of the grief Mileva felt for the effective loss of Lieserl, she fell pregnant again later that year, to her husband's apparent joy. In fact, he greeted the news of the coming child with the curious comment that he had been considering whether he 'shouldn't see to it that you get a new Lieserl'. Whatever Lieserl's fate, Einstein's sentiment behind these words is disquieting.

A son, Hans Albert, was born in 1904, preceding Einstein's incredible creative burst, which included the special theory of relativity. Mileva's role in the *annus mirabilis* has long been a source of contention. She was undoubtedly a gifted physicist and mathematician and it is to be supposed that Einstein shared his ideas with her and that she assisted him with processing data. However, some historians have suggested that Mileva was really the 'power behind the throne', contributing crucial ideas that should have seen her credited as the co-creator of the theory. In reality, there is scant evidence to support such an assertion. What we can be more certain of is that she keenly felt the loss of her own career as her husband's went into the stratosphere.

By 1909, the marriage was in serious trouble. Einstein felt trapped and he treated Mileva with increasing contempt. He was by nature flirtatious with the opposite sex and she had an inherent streak of jealousy. It was an unhappy mix and he would cruelly blame her jealousy on her 'uncommon ugliness'. Several decades later he would tell architect Konrad Wachsmann: 'Marriage makes people treat each other as articles of property and no longer as free human beings.'

But still there was time for another pregnancy, which resulted in the birth of a second son, Eduard, in 1910. By all accounts, Einstein was a good father to them in their early years, although relations with both became more difficult as they got older. After bouncing between academic posts around Europe, the family returned to Zurich in 1912. Living in a large, plush apartment, surrounded by old friends and resuming a settled way of life, this should have been a happy period for the Einsteins, but in fact the marriage was crashing down around their ears.

It was on a visit to Berlin in that year that Einstein became reacquainted with his older cousin, Elsa, with whom he had often played as a child when her family had come to visit his in Munich. Days of childhood innocence gone, they began a dangerous flirtation – although only after Einstein had first made eyes at Elsa's sister. After a lull, the relationship picked up again in 1913 with Einstein charmlessly sending her a note in which he said, 'What I wouldn't give to be able to spend a few days with you, but without my cross.' The cross was, of course, Mileva.

In July of that year, Max Planck and Walther Nernst arrived from Germany in a bid to persuade Einstein that his future lay in Berlin. Their offer was a tempting one. He would be elected to the prestigious Prussian Academy of Sciences and would be given a professorship at the University of Berlin, becoming director of a newly established institute of physics. However, he would not be expected to actively teach, giving him plenty of opportunity to pursue his own scientific interests. He would need to take German citizenship but could keep his Swiss citizenship, too. And to top it all, he was to be handsomely remunerated.

Einstein didn't need his arm twisted much. He saw a chance to 'give [himself] over completely to rumination'. It also meant he could be in close proximity to his new love, Elsa, as well. So it was that the Einsteins were on the move again. It was not long before Elsa was pressing Einstein to demand a divorce from Mileva so that he could marry her. At this stage, however, he was not keen to jump from one marriage straight into another. In fact, he hardly seemed to have time for any family. As Hans Albert would later recall, Einstein gave the impression that his family was taking up too much of his time and distracting him from his work (this was when he was immersed in trying to crack the general theory, let it be remembered). 'I treat my wife as an employee whom I cannot fire,' he would tell a friend. 'I have my own bedroom and avoid being alone with her.'

Mileva, meanwhile, felt increasingly embittered towards her husband, not only because of his ill treatment of her, but for the professional success that he was enjoying and that had eluded her. It is likely that she had some extra-marital dalliances to match his, too. The couple split in July 1914, with Mileva going to stay with mutual friends, the Habers, elsewhere in the city.

At this time, intermediaries like the Habers did their best to resolve the situation. Einstein's contribution was to present Mileva with an extraordinary contract. In it he variously demanded that:

- ⊙ she do his laundry and deliver three meals a day to his room
- ⊙ she tidy his bedroom and study but leave his desk for his sole use
- ⊙ she not expect him to go out with her or sit with her, though they might interact if social demands required it
- ⊙ she not reproach him or expect intimacy, nor talk to him if he asked her not to
- ⊙ she leave his bedroom/study instantly as demanded
- ⊙ she not belittle him to their children

Perhaps the most jaw-dropping aspect of this episode was that Mileva initially went along with it. However, inevitably, a separation was agreed shortly after, with Einstein promising to give his wife and children the equivalent of about half of his income. In late July 1914, Mileva, Hans Albert and Eduard returned to Zurich, with Einstein apparently distraught at the loss of his children. By 1916, Mileva was stricken by awful physical and mental health. The children left the family home to stay with friends but Einstein did not step into the breach.

He repeatedly asked her for a divorce, a request she consistently denied until at last the marriage was formally ended in February 1919. Mileva's later years saw her finances drained by the costs of caring for Eduard, whose mental health problems resulted in his institutionalization. She lived a hard life that had promised so much, and died on 4 August 1948. Had she been alive when *Time* magazine declared her husband 'Person of the Century', she would likely have raised an eyebrow.

Part 2: Elsa Einstein

Although Elsa as the second wife had faced her own difficulties with Einstein, she had him at a different stage in life and was perhaps more of a psychological, if not an intellectual, match for him.

Born in 1876, she had married Max Löwenthal, a textile trader, when she was twenty years old. The union produced three children, two of whom (daughters Ilse and Margot) survived beyond infancy. However, it was not a happy marriage and the couple divorced in 1908, with Elsa and the two girls moving to be close to her parents in Berlin.

By the time she started seeing Einstein, around Easter of 1912, she was thirty-six years old. The pair were first cousins on the maternal side and second cousins on the paternal side. If Einstein was consciously looking for a character different to Mileva, he found her in Elsa. She was not of an intellectual disposition, being inclined instead towards the domestic life. Rather matronly in appearance, she lavished attention on her cousin, which Einstein lapped up. Not shy of declaring his feelings to lovers, he soon wrote to her that he needed 'someone to love, otherwise life is miserable' and telling her that 'this someone is you'.

Elsa longed to settle down with her 'Albertle', as she had called him in childhood. He, though, resisted for a long time. He told her that he would be in no hurry to remarry should he persuade Mileva to divorce him, apprising Elsa that their relationship 'does not have to founder on a provincial narrow-minded lifestyle'. So it was something of a surprise when just four and a half months after he divorced Mileva, he was to be found making his marriage vows to Elsa. She, Albert, Ilse and Margot moved into a large apartment in a smart neighbourhood of Berlin. To the casual onlooker, this was a picture of domestic bourgeois bliss of the type Elsa longed for and Einstein seemingly dreaded.

But if Elsa thought she was in for an easy

ride now she'd got her man, she was wrong. She had to compete for his affections with his work, as well as deal with the attention that accompanied his celebrity status. Meanwhile, in the background swirled the currents of European politics that in the end would drive the couple to relocate to the USA. She also faced the spectre of her husband's infidelity. There was no denying that Einstein found it hard to remain faithful. For a man famous across the planet, there was no shortage of opportunity to test his resolve. In the 1920s he fell in love with his secretary, Betty Neumann, for instance, and Elsa would have undoubtedly been aware of several other affairs. Janos Plesch, Einstein's doctor, is reported to have said: 'Einstein loved women, and the commoner and sweatier and smellier they were, the better he liked them.'

Yet the marriage endured and they seemed broadly content in a way that neither of their first marriages were. Elsa was never less than philosophical about her husband's shortcomings. 'Such a genius should be irreproachable,' she reflected in 1929. 'But nature does not behave this way. Where she gives extravagantly, she takes away extravagantly.' And in a letter written to friends around the same time, she wrote touchingly of the nature of their marriage: 'God has put so much into him that is beautiful, and

I find him wonderful, even though life at his side is debilitating and difficult in every respect.'

In 1935 Elsa was diagnosed with heart and kidney problems. Her health went into a steep and painful decline, and she died on 20 December 1936 at 112 Mercer Street, Princeton, where the Einsteins had made their home in America. What ultimately was her secret to at least partially taming Albert, then, a secret that Mileva could never unlock? 'I manage him,' Elsa once admitted, 'but I never let him know that I manage him.'

Einstein
and God

'A spirit is manifest in the laws of the universe
– a spirit vastly superior to that of man …'

ALBERT EINSTEIN, 1936

The question of Einstein's religious faith, or lack of it, has fascinated observers for the best part of a century. He was asked about his belief in God (or a god) repeatedly throughout his life and spoke often and at some length on the subject. So it is something of an achievement that his position on religion remains so opaque.

Although born into a Jewish family, the Einsteins did not have particularly strong religious convictions. Albert attended a local Catholic school where he was the only Jew in a class of some seventy. It is unfortunate, but perhaps not surprising, given the historical context in which he was living, that he fell victim to the anti-Semitism of some fellow pupils. Indeed, this may have contributed to him developing an unexpected religious zeal after primary school. It was not to last long, though. In his 1946 *Autobiographical Notes*, he wrote of his 'deep religiosity', which came to an 'abrupt ending' when he was twelve years old. 'Through the reading of popular scientific books,' he revealed, 'I soon reached the conviction that much in the stories of the Bible could not be true ... Suspicion against every kind of authority grew out of this experience … an attitude which has never again left me.'

When Max Talmud began introducing him to the works of Kant, Hume and Mach, Einstein was ever more fascinated by their discussions of what we know about reality. He decisively moved away from any traditional religious beliefs in his teens. As he would tell an interviewer for the Japanese magazine *Kaizō 5* in 1922, '"Religious truth" conveys nothing clear to me at all.' However, he began to formulate a complex personal faith that incorporated belief in a higher power and which could be integrated with his own scientific interests.

That Einstein saw a place for both religion and science is clear in his assertion, 'Science without religion is lame; religion without science is blind.' For Einstein, there was no conflict. Both science and religion represented approaches to making sense of existence. For much of history they had been (and often continue to be) in opposition to each other but Einstein saw them as complementary. 'I have found no better expression than "religious" for confidence in the rational nature of reality, insofar as it is accessible to human reason,' he told Maurice Solovine in 1951. 'Whenever this feeling is absent, science degenerates into uninspired empiricism.' On another occasion, he explained to Banesh Hoffman how belief in a divine creator informed his own scientific work: 'I ask myself whether, if I were God, I would have arranged the world in such a way.'

What he did *not* believe in was a bearded God hovering on a cloud, concerned with the affairs of humanity. As he wrote to one correspondent, 'I cannot conceive of a personal God who would directly influence the actions of individuals or would sit in judgement on creatures of his own creation.' In the same letter, he went on to elaborate, 'My religiosity consists of a humble admiration of the infinitely superior spirit that reveals itself in the little that we can comprehend about the knowable world.'

In time he would come to identify most closely with the teachings of Baruch Spinoza, the seventeenth-century Dutch-Jewish philosopher. In his great work, *Ethics*, he broadly outlined a belief not in a personal god but in a theological design to the universe. In 1929 Einstein told *The New York Times*: 'I believe in Spinoza's God, who reveals Himself in the lawful harmony of the world, not in a God who concerns himself with the fate and the doings of mankind.'

The rejection of an 'interfering' God was one he had spoken of before and would return to again. In 1930 he wrote in an article for *The New York Times*:

The man who is thoroughly convinced of the universal operation of the law of causation cannot for a moment entertain the idea of a being who interferes in the course of events ... A God who rewards and punishes is inconceivable to him for the simple reason that a man's actions are determined by necessity, external and internal, so that in God's eyes he cannot be responsible, any more than an inanimate object is responsible for the motions it undergoes …

Instead, time and again he spoke in terms of being able to detect an invisible divine hand through his scientific contemplations. He would describe it thus: 'That deeply emotional conviction of the presence of a superior reasoning power, which is revealed in the incomprehensible universe, forms my idea of God.' He expanded on the subject in an interview with G. S. Viereck:

> Everything is determined … by forces over which we have no control. It is determined for the insect as well as for the star. Human beings, vegetables, or cosmic dust – we all dance to a mysterious tune, intoned in the distance by an invisible piper.

This all chimed with his earlier declaration that his beliefs were 'pantheistic' – that is to say, in accordance with a doctrine that sees the universe as the physical manifestation of the divine.

As he became more assured in his pantheistic outlook, he was in turn increasingly sceptical of the impact of traditional faiths on believers. He was wary of the 'superstition' that he detected among followers of the mainstream religions and believed scientific rationality offered greater hope for the future. In his 1922 *Kaizo 5* interview he said:

Scientific research can reduce superstition by encouraging people to think and view things in terms of cause and effect. It is certain that a conviction akin to a religious feeling, of the rationality or intelligibility of the world lies behind all scientific work of a higher order.

Some two decades later he was making much the same argument. In 1940 he spoke at a New York symposium on 'Science, Philosophy and Religion':

The further the spiritual evolution of mankind advances, the more certain it seems to me that the path to genuine religiosity does not lie through the fear of life, and the fear of death, and blind faith, but through striving after rational knowledge.

Ultimately, Einstein did not hold with religion based on ancient scriptures or a fearful contemplation of the afterlife. It was rooted in the same instincts that drove his science: a fascination with the mysterious workings of the world and the universe and a faith that those mysteries may ultimately be explained. He spoke no more elegantly on the subject than in an article he wrote in 1930 for the periodical *Forum and Century* entitled 'What I Believe':

The most beautiful thing we can experience is the mysterious. It is the source of all true art and science.

He to whom this emotion is a stranger, who can no longer pause to wonder and stand rapt in awe, is as good as dead: his eyes are closed. This insight into the mystery of life, coupled though it be with fear, has also given rise to religion. To know that what is impenetrable to us really exists, manifesting itself as the highest wisdom and the most radiant beauty which our dull faculties can comprehend only in their most primitive forms – this knowledge, this feeling, is at the centre of true religiousness. In this sense, and in this sense only, I belong in the ranks of devoutly religious men.

This all flew in the face of a belief widely held in Einstein's own lifetime that he represented the triumph of science over religion. The theory of relativity had overthrown long-held 'certainties' and seemed to challenge accepted religious doctrines as effectively as Darwin's ideas had the previous century. It was unsurprising, then, that Einstein would become a figurehead for certain adherents of atheism. However, this was a status that he explicitly rejected.

In fact, he found atheism disquieting when it took the form of a proactive movement and he was keen to distance himself from it. In the early 1940s in a conversation with the anti-Nazi German diplomat Hubertus zu Löwenstein, he spoke of his anger at those people who say there is no God and 'quote me for support of such views'. A couple of years before he died, he would explain: 'What separates me from most so-called atheists is a feeling of utter humility toward the unattainable secrets of the harmony of the cosmos.'

It was assertive atheism's refusal to countenance that it might itself be wrong that seemed to have offended him most. In our own time, aggressive atheism is an unironic advocate of a religious fervour in those with an unshakeable faith in its doctrines. Such posturing riled Einstein, prompting him to complain that 'there are the fanatical atheists whose intolerance is the same as that of the religious fanatics, and it springs from the same source', before dismissing them as 'creatures who can't hear the music of the spheres'.

There was a further complication to consider when trying to get to the bottom of just what Einstein believed: how could he reconcile his belief in the causal determinism of the universe with his demand that humanity take moral responsibility for its actions? His scientific background left him in no doubt that everything that happens in the universe is predetermined by natural laws and the accumulated impact of what has already happened. It thus leaves no room for events to be influenced by human free will and so renders the notion of moral responsibility redundant. In 1932 he told the Spinoza Society, 'Human beings in their thinking, feeling and acting are not free but are as causally bound as the stars in their motions.'

Yet Einstein did expect good from people and, as shall be seen in later sections of this book, called for a politics in which individuals made ethically guided choices. While he did not accept the reality of free will, he recognized the usefulness of the notion as a social tool. People must, he saw, be required to take responsibility for their actions in order that society might be civil. He explained it in these terms to G. S. Viereck: 'I know that philosophically a murderer is not responsible for his crime, but I prefer not to take tea with him.'

In practical terms, this meant that he called on others to behave decently. For instance, he urged restraint and charity to his step-daughters, telling them, 'Use for yourself little but give to others much.' Meanwhile, to Cornelius Greenway, a New York vicar, he would say, 'Only morality in our actions can give beauty and dignity to life.' While Einstein broadly rejected the doctrines of the great religions, he saw in their figureheads models for humanitarianism. It was an idea he explored in a statement in 1937: 'What humanity owes to personalities like Buddha, Moses, and Jesus ranks for me higher than all the achievements of the inquiring constructive mind.'

So Einstein's take on religion was in some respects very straightforward and in others enormously complex. He was, furthermore, well aware of the contradictory nature of his position, as when he told a friend shortly before his death: 'I am a deeply religious non-believer ... this is somewhat a new kind of religion.'

EINSTEIN, JUDAISM AND ZIONISM

'As much as I feel myself to be a Jew, I stand aloof from the traditional religious rites.'

ALBERT EINSTEIN TO THE JEWISH
COMMUNITY OF BERLIN, 1920

Although Einstein was never a religiously observant Jew, bar a brief phase in his youth, he always felt a part of the wider Jewish community, and increasingly so as he got older. Though it is curious to contemplate it, he seems to have felt a growing sense of his Jewishness even as his personal religious beliefs diverged from those of the traditional Abrahamic religions. In old age he would say that 'my relationship to the Jewish people has become my strongest human tie'.

After his brief dalliance with established religion in his late pre-teen years, Einstein refused to identify himself as of the Jewish religion. By 1896, when he rendered himself officially stateless, he was describing himself as of 'no religious denomination' in official documentation. When he accepted a job at the University of Prague in 1910, he was required to take Austro–Hungarian citizenship, which in turn meant it was necessary for him to profess a religion. He eventually opted for the designation 'Mosaic' (which is to say, of beliefs related to the teachings of Moses; a term sometimes used as a somewhat archaic synonym for Judaism). He used the term again on his divorce papers in 1919, but only after he had suggested 'dissenter' as his preferred term.

But the rise in anti-Semitism in the 1920s, especially in his native Germany, reconnected Einstein with his Jewish cultural heritage, though not with Judaism's religious rites. 'There is nothing in me that can be described as a "Jewish faith",' he would say. 'However, I am happy to be a member of the Jewish people.' Such proclamations inevitably garnered hostility from some quarters. In 1920, for instance, a crankish organization going under the name of the Study Group of German Scientists for the Preservation of a Pure Science attacked him on the grounds that he had financially benefited from his work on relativity and condemned the 'Jewish nature' of his theory.

If the perpetrators hoped such tactics would silence Einstein, they were sadly misguided. The stronger the tide of anti-Semitism, the more he embraced his Jewishness. Sigmund Freud, another of the great Jewish intellectuals of the twentieth century, theorized about how Jewish scientists displayed a 'creative scepticism' inherent in the historic outsider status of Jews in Europe.

Appalled by the rise of European fascism, Einstein responded with an ever stouter defence of his Jewish brothers and sisters. It is telling that in 1921 he agreed to accompany Chaim Weizmann, president of the World Zionist Organization, on a tour to the USA in order to raise funds for a proposed Jewish university in Palestine. In the same year, Hitler was complaining that German science, 'once our greatest pride', was now being taught 'by Hebrews'.

The link-up with Weizmann was nonetheless surprising, given Einstein's innate distrust of nationalism. But even if he did not share Weizmann's desire for a Jewish state at this point in time, he was attracted by the thought of a culturally Jewish sense of 'nation' and was specifically attracted to helping establish what would become Jerusalem's Hebrew University. The tour itself was nothing short of spectacular. Einstein received the sort of welcome that had been reserved for Charles Dickens eighty years earlier and which was unleashed on The Beatles forty years later.

Yet the situation in Europe was only getting worse. Hyperinflation in Germany fanned the flames of anti-Jewish sentiment and in 1922 Germany's Jewish foreign minister, Walter Rathenau, was savagely assassinated in a nationalist attack. He was shot in his car before a grenade was thrown into the vehicle. The crime profoundly shocked Einstein, who was warned by the police that he too was at risk. Fame, he concluded, had 'set the rabble against me'.

Throughout the rise of Hitler, the Second World War and the horrors of the Holocaust, Einstein clung to his Jewishness but remained ambivalent on the question of a Jewish state, the goal of the Zionists. He stated that his heart was never truly behind the idea and he feared that Judaism might be damaged by what he described as a 'narrow nationalism'. While he championed the fight against anti-Semitism, he argued that he could not see the need for a separate homeland.

He felt disquiet at the sometimes militaristic rhetoric from some quarters of the Zionist movement. In 1948, for instance, he signed a petition that denounced Menachem Begin – a future president of the nation – as a terrorist. However, with the birth of the State of Israel that same year, Einstein realized that the point of no return had been reached. Though he had opposed state creation 'for economic, political and military reasons', he knew that the fight was now to ensure sound foundations.

This principally meant peaceful integration with the indigenous Arab population, whom he believed had been too long neglected by those intent on birthing Israel. As far back as 1929 he had spoken to Hugo Bergmann, philosophy professor at the Hebrew University of Jerusalem, of his belief that all Jewish children in Palestine should learn Arabic. In the same year, he said to Chaim Weizmann: 'Should we be unable to find a way to honest cooperation and honest pacts with the Arabs, then we have learned absolutely nothing from our 2,000 years of suffering and will deserve our fate.'

Having grown up in a time and place where he had suffered persecution for his cultural heritage, his desire was for a society of equals. Shortly before he died, he set out his vision to Zvi Lurie, one of the signatories to Israel's declaration of independence:

> The most important aspect of our policy must be our ever-present, manifest desire to institute complete equality for the Arab citizens living in our midst ... The attitude we adopt toward the Arab minority will provide the real test of our moral standards as a people.

Given his complicated feelings towards Israel, it was little surprise when in 1952 he rejected the opportunity to become the nation's president following the death of the incumbent, Weizmann. The Prime Minister, David Ben-Gurion, felt that he had little choice but to offer him the post given the weight of public opinion supporting the appointment. But to the relief of all the key players, the US-based Einstein gracefully refused, believing (almost certainly correctly) that he lacked both the required natural aptitude and the experience. In a phone call with the Israeli ambassador in Washington, he stated, 'I am not the person for that and I cannot possibly do it.'

Einstein's life was most certainly informed by his Jewishness, but in the end he refused to let it or any other cultural designation define him. As he told the German mathematician, Adolf Kneser, in 1918: 'I am by heritage a Jew, by citizenship a Swiss, and by disposition a human being, and *only* a human being, without any special attachment to any state or national entity whatsoever.'

Perhaps his feelings towards his own non-religious Jewishness are best summed up in the words of an article he wrote for *Colliers* magazine twenty years later: 'The bond that has united the Jews for thousands of years and that unites them today is, above all, the democratic ideal of social justice coupled with the ideal of mutual aid and tolerance among all men.'

Take Time
to Unwind

'He sailed like Odysseus.'

MARGOT EINSTEIN
(ALBERT'S STEP-DAUGHTER)

Einstein threw himself into his work with ferocious intensity and was not known as someone who liked to relax through a wide range of hobbies. Indeed, his friend Alice Kahler once revealed that among his few favoured pastimes was puzzle solving, which seems to the onlooker like a serious case of 'busman's holiday'. She recalled how on one occasion she gave him a gift of a Chinese cross (an interlocking, three-dimensional puzzle) – a notoriously taxing challenge. Somewhat disappointingly for Kahler, Einstein solved it within three minutes.

So what did he do to relax? Well, though it may not have been quite what the doctor ordered, he did enjoy pipe smoking (as well as the occasional cigar, much to the displeasure of his second wife). Through the plumes of smoke, Einstein was sure that the world came into sharper focus. Such was his commitment to the enterprise that in 1950 he was awarded an honorary life membership of the Montreal Pipe Smokers Club. In response to the accolade, he commented: 'Pipe-smoking contributes to a somewhat calm and objective judgement in all human affairs.'

More healthily, he was also a keen sailor, an activity he first seriously got to grips with as a student on the lakes around Zurich. Its attractions were manifold, but prominent among them was the opportunity for tranquillity. Not for Einstein the frantic action of competitive sailing; instead he regarded it as 'the sport that demands the least energy'. It is fair to say he was less Ben Ainslie and more Ratty from *The Wind in the Willows*. Although he did sail with friends, he often went unaccompanied, glorying in the chance for some solitary reflection away from his desk and from the demands of other people.

Sailing represented a rare chance for complete freedom. Such was his feeling of liberation that he even refused to wear a life jacket despite being a poor swimmer. It was an interest he pursued with vigour after he had moved to the USA, often relocating in the summer to places chosen with sailing in mind. He eventually bought himself a seventeen-foot wooden boat, which he named *Tinef* (Yiddish for 'piece of junk'). The delight he took in his time on the water is evident in a letter he wrote in 1954 to Elisabeth, by then the Queen Mother of Belgium:

Sailing in the secluded coves of the coast here is more than relaxing … I have a compass that shines in the dark, like a serious seafarer. But I am not so talented in this art, and I am satisfied if I can manage to get myself off the sandbanks on which I become lodged.

It is interesting to note, too, his ongoing fascination with the compass, the device that first captivated him as a young boy.

One year Einstein summered in Rhode Island and took every opportunity he could to set sail on the ocean wave. A local yacht club member would recall years later how the great man would go off for days at a time, seemingly floating adrift. On several occasions rescue parties were sent out to save him only to find Einstein aboard his boat in a state of contented contemplation. As his fame and celebrity spread, the water increasingly served as a place where he could be himself once more – not Einstein the genius, the discoverer of relativity, the personality with the crazy hair. Margot Einstein summed it up best as she reflected in 1978: 'When one was with him on the sailboat, you felt him as an element. He had something so natural and strong in him because he was himself a piece of nature.'

THE VIOLIN VIRTUOSO

'If I were not a physicist, I would probably be a musician.'

ALBERT EINSTEIN, 1929

However great his love of sailing, his grandest passion was reserved for music. It was an affection instilled in him by his mother, who coerced him into taking violin lessons, and he came to adore both the production and consumption of music. 'I often think in music. I live my daydreams in music. I see my life in terms of music ... I get most joy in life out of my violin,' he told G. S. Viereck in 1929.

Mozart was the object of his greatest admiration. Einstein admired the simplicity of his compositions (simplicity being at the base of all that was beautiful in his view) and their purity, which he regarded 'as a reflection of the inner beauty of the universe itself'. Just behind Mozart came Bach, with Einstein in awe at the way that the music of both men seemed to have arrived already fully formed rather than consciously composed. Schubert, meanwhile, met with his approval for the powerful communication of emotion, though he found Beethoven's work so rawly personal that it left him feeling uncomfortable. He was decidedly less enamoured of Handel, Wagner and Mendelssohn, which gives an indication of the high musical bar he set.

Einstein himself was a more than competent violinist who needed little persuading to perform in public. During his time studying in Aarau, he played a series of local church concerts, and once he was established as a major global figure he would give concerts to raise funds for one or other of his favoured causes. At a fundraiser in Manhattan in the 1930s he played Bach and Mozart, with *Time* noting that he 'became so absorbed in the music that with a faraway look he was still plucking at the strings when the performance was all over'.

There were plenty of private recitals too, to which the members of the Olympia Academy and even the King and Queen of Belgium could attest. Not everyone was entirely complimentary about his skills, though. The professional musician Walter Friedrich, for instance, commented in the late 1920s that 'Einstein's fiddling was like that of a lumberjack sawing a log'. But others clearly saw the seeds of genuine talent. Just take a rather curious review of one of his performances from the early 1920s, whose author concluded: 'Einstein's playing is excellent, but he does not deserve his world fame; there are many others just as good.' The reviewer was apparently oblivious to the fact that Einstein's fame was rooted rather more in his scientific endeavours, thus giving the opportunity for this extraordinary backhanded compliment.

Einstein often turned to his fiddle when confronted with a particularly knotty problem, in the manner of Sherlock Holmes. Friends reported how he could sometimes be found strolling around his kitchen and playing the instrument, only stopping to exclaim that he had solved his conundrum. As he entered old age, he played the violin rarely, spending more time at the piano despite being a less skilled player. Nonetheless, it shows the importance he placed on music throughout his life. As he noted in 1928: 'Music does not influence research work, but both are nourished by the same sort of longing, and they complement each other in the satisfaction they offer.'

How to Eat
Like Einstein

'I am often so engrossed in my work
that I forget to eat lunch.'

ALBERT EINSTEIN

A lthough he was fêted around the world in the latter decades of his life, Einstein remained a man of mostly modest tastes. He believed that plain living was good for both body and soul.

Crippled by a lack of money, the dinners conducted by the Olympia Academy were typically humble affairs. Sausages were a staple, along with cheese (gruyère being a particular favourite) and fruit, all washed down with tea. Macaroni was always well received; a taste no doubt consolidated by his spells living in Italy, and it is also known that he was partial to an ice cream cone. There is also a record of a fairly basic meal he enjoyed with the King and Queen of Belgium that consisted of spinach, fried egg and potatoes.

In selecting a menu, Einstein was forced to consider the stomach problems he developed in 1917 that caused him to lose several stone and plagued him for the rest of his life. Believed to have been caused partly by the nutritional shortfalls of a wartime diet, he was subsequently instructed to follow a carbohydrate-heavy diet. However, he lived alone in that period and struggled to follow his doctor's orders to the long-term detriment of his health.

He also flirted with vegetarianism at various stages of his life, although he found it difficult to entirely turn his back on meat. 'I have always eaten animal flesh with a somewhat guilty conscience,' he confided in 1953. Yet he had previously spoken of 'agreeing with the aims of vegetarianism for aesthetic and moral reasons' and believed that both the physiological and temperamental effects of a vegetarian diet improved 'the lot of mankind'. Medically required to forgo meat, fish and fats in the year before his death, he would reflect: 'It almost seems to me that man was not born to be a carnivore.'

Nor was he an enthusiastic consumer of alcohol, as bluntly revealed in the response he gave to a question about his attitude to prohibition, which operated in the USA from 1920 until 1933: 'I don't drink, so I couldn't care less.' However, despite his health problems, he was not teetotal, preferring wine and cognac to other forms of alcohol. But given the whirl of social functions he was asked to attend, it is perhaps fortunate that he would typically only sup at the innumerable glasses of liquor forced into his hand.

Think Big

'He knew, as did Socrates, that we know nothing.'

MAX BORN, SPEAKING AFTER THE DEATH
OF EINSTEIN, 1955

While a lesser man and a lesser mind might have been content to wallow in the glories of outlining the special theory of relativity, within two years of publishing his game-changing paper Einstein was turning his mind to an even more complex problem. It is one of his most notable characteristics that he refused to impose any limits on what mankind might know and, as a result, insisted on posing boundless challenges to himself.

Even as the rest of the world was only just beginning to come to terms with the revelations contained within the special theory, Einstein was obsessing over its shortfalls. Specifically, he was unhappy that it applied only under circumstances of motion at constant velocity. Furthermore, Newton's universe relied on the notion that gravity is an instantaneous force but Einstein realized this could not be right since he had established that nothing could travel faster than the speed of light.

In a way that was now becoming familiar, his first great breakthrough came via a thought experiment centred on the sensations experienced by a person free falling while contained in an enclosed space such as an elevator. However, it would take him a further eight gruelling years to complete the general theory, during which he worked, by his own admission, 'horrendously intensely'.

One of the chief problems he faced was that his theory required new types of mathematics. For starters, he needed a form of geometry that went beyond that which Euclid had defined, the basics of which most of us are taught at school. While perfect for describing a three-dimensional world, it frankly wasn't up to the job for Einstein. So he turned to his old student chum from Zurich (and subsequently the institution's professor of descriptive geometry), Marcel Grossmann. Einstein had pleaded with him, '… you've got to help me or I will go crazy'. Grossmann came up trumps, guiding Einstein through swathes of complex mathematics and directing him to the non-Euclidean calculations of Bernhard Riemann, who had devised systems to discern distances between points in space regardless of how much that space was contorted. The calculus of the Italian Gregorio Ricci-Curbastro was also crucial in the development of new tensors (highly intricate mathematical constructions suited for use in multi-dimensions).

By the end of 1915, Einstein was confident that he had suitably refined his theory and had the maths to back it up. Over a series of four lectures that year he laid out what he considered to be 'the most valuable discovery of my life'. Four years later, the first observable evidence for his postulations were made and overnight he went from being a well-known figure of modern science to a global superstar whose name carried weight in even the least scientific households.

His fame spread despite the inability of the vast majority of the population to grasp the essence of the science he had laid out. Chaim Weizmann encapsulated the widespread confusion that surrounded the general theory when he reflected on the voyage he made with Einstein from Europe to the USA in 1921. 'During our crossing,' he wryly observed, 'Einstein explained his theory to me every day, and by the time we arrived I was fully convinced he understood it.'

However, if the maths and the scientific discourse was baffling to most, its broad implications were easier to grasp – a fact that Einstein, always blessed with a populist streak, understood well. In the same year that he had travelled across the Atlantic with Weizmann, he spoke to *The New York Times* about relativity:

The practical man need not worry ... From the philosophical aspect, however, it has importance, as it alters the conceptions of time and space which are necessary to philosophical speculations and conceptions.

There were times when Einstein found the general theory, or at least the questions it raised and the attention it garnered him, burdensome. Six years after the theory's publication, he would comment to Elsa: 'I'm now pretty much fed up with relativity! Even such a thing wears thin when one becomes too preoccupied with it.' But it was unrealistic to think that such a momentous achievement wouldn't cast a shadow over the rest of his life. No one ever said that thinking big was easy, after all.

In the final reckoning, though, Einstein had wanted to better understand the 'harmony of the cosmos' and that is just what he achieved. In an article entitled 'What is the theory of relativity?' and published in *The Times* in 1919, his achievements were summed up thus: 'His clear and wide-ranging ideas will retain their unique significance for all time as the foundation of our whole modern conceptual structure in the sphere of natural philosophy.' Acclaim indeed.

THE GENERAL THEORY OF RELATIVITY

'Compared with this problem, the original theory of relativity is child's play.'

ALBERT EINSTEIN, 1912

When he was asked to sum up the general theory in a single sentence (a question that plagued him wherever journalists followed), Einstein retorted: 'All of my life I have been trying to get it into one book and he wants me to get it into one sentence.' Nonetheless he gave it a go, describing it as 'a theory of space and time, as far as physics is concerned, which leads to a theory of gravitation'. It is, all things considered, not a bad overview.

By 1907, Einstein was thinking deeply about the weaknesses he saw in his special theory. His thoughts were ever focused on the general and the universal, rather than on laws that applied only under specific conditions. As we saw earlier, he began to turn over in his mind the idea of a person in free fall in an enclosed box. At a lecture delivered in Japan in 1922 he related the details of his 'Eureka!' moment:

I was sitting in the Patent Office in Bern when all of a sudden a thought occurred to me: if a person falls freely, he won't feel his own weight. I was startled. This simple thought made a deep impression on me. It impelled me toward a theory of gravitation.

Imagine a person in an elevator free falling towards earth – they would float freely inside the elevator, and if they removed their watch from their wrist, that too would float freely beside them. It would feel to the person as if they were in an elevator sitting still in zero gravity. Equally, if the elevator was speeding up through space without feeling the pull of gravity, the subject inside would be pushed to the floor just as if they were being pulled by gravity. Traditionally, gravity and acceleration were regarded as different phenomena, although both related to mass. Einstein's great insight was to realize that gravitational mass and inertial mass are equivalent – an idea that he called the 'equivalence principle'. Having come to this conclusion, Einstein now potentially had the tools to extend the special theory so that it related to accelerated systems and not just to scenarios of constant velocity.

Another implication of his thought experiment was that gravity could bend light. If you took the free-falling elevator and pierced a hole in one side, a beam of light would hit the opposite wall at a higher point than that at which it entered. Its trajectory has been bent. It was this understanding that light did not, as was previously thought, always travel in straight lines that called for a new system of geometry, since Euclidean geometry was great for dealing with flat surfaces but inadequate when dealing with curvatures.

The general theory accordingly describes how gravity is a warping of time and space. Einstein's great challenge – the reason he spent so long polishing the theory – was to find the maths to explain just how gravity acts on matter and how matter generates gravity in the space–time realm. To get an idea of how this works, consider rolling a bowling ball on to a trampoline. The fabric of the trampoline bends as the ball travels across it and comes to rest. Now add another bowling ball into the picture. It rolls and comes to rest next to the first ball. Does the first ball exert a mysterious force to draw the second ball to it? No – the two balls lie next to each other on account of the warping of the trampoline fabric. The general theory laid out the field equations to explain how much the same happens in space–time. Simple, eh?

In short, where Newton described a universe in which an apple falls to the ground from a tree because gravity exerts a force of attraction, Einstein redefined gravity as a curvature of space–time. He explained his *magnum opus* to his younger son, Eduard, like this: 'When a blind beetle crawls over the surface of a curved branch, it doesn't notice that the track it has covered is indeed curved. I was lucky enough to notice what the beetle didn't notice.'

In his 1917 paper 'Cosmological Considerations in the General Theory of Relativity', Einstein envisaged a universe that was at once finite and unbounded, a condition made possible by imagining it endlessly curving back in on itself. Among myriad implications, the general theory allowed us to begin to understand the phenomena of black holes (though Einstein at the time was unconvinced of their existence) and wormholes, and even to speculate on how the Big Bang occurred.

However, getting to that stage was at times excruciating. 'Nature hides her secret because of her essential loftiness, but not by means of ruse,' Einstein said in one of his more philosophical moments, but now and again he must have felt like everything was working against him. For instance, as early as 1911 he had predicted that the sun's gravity could bend starlight. The problem was that no one could prove this in the absence of a solar eclipse. As good luck would have it, one was due on 21 August 1914, but then bad luck interceded in the form of the onset of the First World War. The opportunity to prove his hypothesis disappeared, and would not reappear for another five years. (In 1919 a research party led by the British astronomer Arthur Eddington travelled to Príncipe, an island in West Africa, at the time of a solar eclipse and made the necessary observations to prove Einstein right.)

Einstein continued with his arduous work even as the war raged around him in Europe. As he was struggling with the principle of equivalence in 1914, he told Heinrich Zangger: 'Nature shows us only the tail of the lion. But I have no doubt that the lion belongs with it even if he cannot reveal himself all at once. We see him only the way a louse that sits upon him would.'

Sure enough, by late 1915 he had cracked the mysteries of the general theory, unpicking the interactions that make up the complex relationships between space, time, energy and matter. He himself would describe the theory as of 'incomparable beauty'. Newton's world fixed time and space, with gravity an almost mystical force of attraction operating separately from them. In Einstein's world, space–time was both changed by and altered gravity, so imposing its own influence on the objects and events dwelling within its dominion. Max Born would describe the theory as nothing less than 'the greatest feat of human thinking about nature – the most amazing combination of philosophical penetration, physical intuition and mathematical skill.'

Back Yourself

'The Nobel Prize – in the event of the divorce
and the event that it is bestowed upon me –
would be ceded to you in full.'

ALBERT EINSTEIN, 1918

As evidenced by the tenacity he displayed in formulating the general theory, Einstein was able to deal with difficulties and setbacks with enormous fortitude. An instinctive belief he was going in the right direction with his ideas was invaluable in this respect.

There is little to suggest that Einstein ever struggled with self-confidence in a significant way. From youth, he was happy to carve his own path through life, pursuing his distinctive interests and unafraid to make big statements of intent, such as his decision to surrender his German citizenship in only his late teens. In adulthood, he forged healthy relationships with a broad range of friends and colleagues and, as we have seen in grim detail, had little problem bonding with the opposite sex.

The quotation above represents arguably the most flamboyant demonstration of bravado of his life. He made the offer to Mileva in 1918 after years of being denied a divorce (an indication of his longing for a formal separation). By February 1919 their split had been formalized, and by 1922 she had the cash in her account. Although today we recognize that it would have been a travesty had he never received the Nobel Prize, there can have been few candidates before or since so certain of their position that they have pre-empted its awarding quite so brazenly.

Yet in pushing the boundaries of human knowledge, Einstein endured many dark nights of the soul. He discussed the agony and ecstasy of his working life in a lecture he gave at the University of Glasgow in 1933:

> The years of anxious searching in the dark for a truth that one feels but cannot express, the intense desire and the alternations of confidence and misgiving until one achieves clarity and understanding, can be understood only by those who have experienced them.

His success as a theoretical physicist was in no little part down to his willingness to stick to his guns when others might have been thrown off course by setbacks and disappointments. However, that did not mean continuing on blindly when all the evidence pointed to needing a change in direction. Einstein accepted that he would make mistakes (working on the furthest frontiers of understanding, it was inevitable), but more importantly, he would learn from them, whether that meant slightly tweaking his approach or starting again from scratch.

This was the case in the near decade that elapsed between Einstein turning his attention to the formulation of the general theory and its final publication. In that time, he was forced to explore entirely new systems of mathematics (a discipline that we know did not always come easily to him), never losing heart when one approach failed and he had to take up a new one.

Nor was he too proud to seek help when required. There is a strong suggestion that part of the reason that Einstein explored seemingly unconventional ideas long after others may have retreated from them was because he so often worked alone. It was as if he was able to remain confident that his underlying convictions were right because he was not surrounded by other people casting doubt on them. But when the situation demanded it, he was happy to turn to those who could facilitate the progression of his work. For instance, in 1915 he became convinced that the maths he was using was flawed. 'I do not believe I am able to find the mistake myself,' he told Michele Besso, 'for in this matter my mind is too deep set in a rut.'

As well as dealing with his own demons, his spreading fame also forced him to confront questions and criticisms from a public and media that all too often did not understand the true implications of his work. For instance, a 1919 editorial column in *The New York Times* (a paper that over the long term was largely supportive of Einstein) suggested that the general theory had the potential to undermine the very foundations of human thought. Then there were those who wilfully misrepresented him, often for ideological reasons of their own. In addition, the scientific community naturally probed at his theories, some driven by genuine scientific inquisitiveness but others more eager to undermine a professional rival.

His resolve was perhaps most severely tested in the post-general theory phase of his career as he attempted to come up with a unified field theory – an enterprise that lacked the forward momentum of his earlier ventures. Yet, through it all, he persevered in exploring the science he intuitively felt gave the best chance of breaking new ground.

Nor was Einstein ever one to undersell himself. Although desire for material gain played little part in his career, he enjoyed a comfortable standard of living and negotiated fair prices for his services, whether it be taking up a professorship or giving a one-off lecture. Given the uncertainly he experienced at the start of his career, who can blame him for wanting to achieve a certain level of security?

However, there was the odd occasion when even Einstein's self-assuredness wavered. In applying the general theory to the universe as a whole in 1917, he devised a 'cosmological constant' that he believed would help explain why the cosmos had not shrunk into a small dense blob. Later he would retract it, describing it as the 'biggest blunder' of his life. Today the constant is back in vogue, a potent weapon in the battle to understand the expansion of the universe. Even a genius is allowed to have the wobbles once in a while, and it just goes to show that some people's mistakes are more important than others' greatest achievements.

THE NOBEL PRIZE

'Einstein stands above his contemporaries
even as Newton did.'

ARTHUR EDDINGTON

The saga of the awarding of the Nobel Prize to Einstein is an occasionally surprising tale that did not always reflect well on the scientific community. Rather, it serves to illustrate just how revolutionary Einstein's work was and encapsulates some of the peculiar challenges he confronted, including opposition fuelled by anti-Semitism.

Einstein was awarded the 1921 Nobel Prize, but not until 1922. This was because the Nobel committee in 1921 had decided that no nominees met the criteria of Alfred Nobel's will. So, why the delay? In 1921 Einstein had been nominated, as you might expect, for his work on relativity. But the awarding committee was unable to reach agreement as to whether his theory qualified, as under Nobel rules it needed to be classed as a 'discovery or invention'. There was a vocal body that argued that the theory lacked sufficient experimental proof to describe it as a 'law' that had been 'discovered', rather than as a 'theory' that had been 'proposed'. This, despite Eddington's solar eclipse observations two years earlier, which had been widely accepted as proof of Einstein's hypothesis.

Einstein had been first nominated for a Nobel Prize back in 1910 by Wilhelm Ostwald of Leipzig University, who himself had become a Nobel laureate the previous year. It was a notable nomination for the fact that Ostwald had been one of the academics who had not even responded to a direct plea from Einstein for a job a decade earlier (and it is to Ostwald's credit that he realized he had been too hasty in dismissing the young scientist). Twelve years on, the Nobel committee simply could not continue to ignore the man who was by now the most famous scientist alive. The Frenchman Marcel Brillouin, who also proposed Einstein for the award in 1922, pointed out how it would seem fifty years down the line if he continued to be overlooked. Realizing that a failure to acknowledge Einstein would be to the detriment of the Nobel brand, a compromise was made.

Carl Wilhelm Oseen had joined the Nobel committee in 1922 and was able to intervene in what was becoming an impasse. The campaign to deny Einstein the prize was led by relativity sceptics, so he decided to take relativity out of the equation, so to speak. Instead, he suggested Einstein be honoured for what the official citation called 'his services to theoretical physics, and especially for his discovery of the law of the photoelectric effect'. Therefore, Einstein never won a Nobel prize for his general theory, but instead for the first of his 1905 papers, 'On a Heuristic Viewpoint Concerning the Production and Transformation of Light'.

There was a certain irony in this, since that study owed a great deal to Philipp Lenard, himself a Nobel laureate and perhaps the most vocal of those attempting to prevent Einstein receiving a prize. This was driven in large part by anti-Semitism, which eventually saw him decry Einstein at rallies and condemn what he called 'Jewish physics'. The Nobel committee received a single letter of protest after Einstein won the 1922 award, and Lenard was its author.

By the time Einstein was made a laureate, he had grown understandably tired of the whole process. He did not attend the award ceremony, being on tour in Japan. However, he did make good on the clause in his divorce settlement, depositing the 121,572 Swedish kronor in the bank account of his ex-wife, Mileva. It was used to finance the purchase of three homes in Zurich.

Swim Against the Tide

'What is truly valuable in our bustle of life is …
the creative and impressionable individuality, the
personality – he who produces the noble and sublime
while the common herd remains dull in thought
and insensible in feeling.'

ALFRED EINSTEIN, 1930

It was a hallmark of his life that Einstein rarely lusted after mainstream acceptance, and often found himself somewhat isolated. Indeed, he frequently seemed most comfortable as an outsider, which contributed to his readiness to follow his instincts in directions that seemed to go against the consensus. Looking back on his life in 1953, he described himself as an 'incorrigible non-conformist'.

It was a trait evident from very early on. His school-teachers and university professors regularly found him a handful as he kicked against the constraints of formal education. His core belief in the superiority of the individual saw him rub up against all types of institutionalization, from school and political party to nation state and established religion.

In his professional life, he made a career of fearlessly ignoring scientific orthodoxy. Even in his personal life, he chose long-term partners who largely failed to conform with others' expectations and aspirations for him. Marlon Brando in the 1953 movie *The Wild One* was asked, 'Hey Johnny, what are you rebelling against?', to which he memorably replied, 'Whadda you got?' Einstein might have shared much the same sentiment.

However, he tempered his inclination to forge ahead on his own distinctive paths with a willingness to retreat and reassess if he suspected he had made a misstep. He did not act with the specific aim of undermining orthodoxy. Rather, he followed the evidence of his own thought processes wherever they led him, whether they conformed to accepted norms or not. If new evidence subsequently suggested he needed to change his mindset, on any matter, he would. There was no hypocrisy in this. He was a scientist, after all, and felt no shame in altering tack in response to what the facts were telling him.

Einstein's tendency to swim against the tide was, in actuality, rooted in his desire to relentlessly question and probe in the search for truth and order. In that sense, he was remarkably orthodox, since, like any scientist, his greatest desire was to uncover the rules that govern everything. After Einstein's death, the editor William Miller recalled him speaking these words:

The important thing is not to stop questioning. Curiosity has its own reasons for existing. One cannot help but be in awe when one contemplates the mysteries of eternity, of life, of the marvellous structure of reality. It is enough if one tries to comprehend only a little of this mystery every day.

EINSTEIN'S BATTLE WITH QUANTUM MECHANICS

'I must seem like an ostrich who forever buries its head in the relativistic sand in order not to face the evil quanta.'

ALBERT EINSTEIN, 1954

Einstein's relationship with quantum mechanics offers a perfect example of his propensity to operate against prevailing trends. Quantum theory represents arguably the greatest paradox of his life: on one hand Einstein was key to the revolution that birthed it; on the other hand, he spent decades poking holes in it.

His 1905 paper on light quanta armed the likes of Max Planck with the evidence they had been searching for to support the development of quantum mechanics – a body of principles that tries to explain how matter and energy behave at the atomic and sub-atomic levels. Key to quantum theory is the notion that matter may be both particle and wave at the same time (wave–particle duality). Previously, this had been thought impossible.

The science behind this discovery is startling, but not nearly so much as some of its implications. Even Einstein struggled to make sense of what it all meant. But after years of development involving armies of scientists around the world, a broadly accepted quantum code emerged in the 1920s and 1930s. Einstein found much of it deeply disquieting.

Having played a pivotal role in describing the phenomenon of light quanta, he understood it pointed the way towards a new science. At a conference in Salzburg in 1909, he acknowledged that quantum physics would dominate 'the next phase of theoretical physics'. However, by the time of the famous 1911 Solvay Conference in Brussels – regarded as a landmark moment in the development of quantum theory – he was already starting to voice a certain cynicism even as many of his colleagues were embracing it. The following year he would tell Heinrich Zangger: 'The more successes the quantum theory enjoys, the sillier it looks.'

Where Einstein longed for firm rules that explained the reality of the universe, quantum theory seemed intent on dispensing with them – one of its founding tenets, let's not forget, is the uncertainty principle. Einstein believed in a deterministic world where everything happens for a reason. Now the prevailing quantum orthodoxy was that the world is governed by uncertainty and chance, and that there is no objective reality. Einstein's response was to claim that 'God does not play dice'. It was a statement that once prompted Niels Bohr, leading light of the influential Copenhagen interpretation of quantum mechanics, to playfully tell Einstein to stop telling God what to do. Einstein and Bohr, respectful admirers of each other both professionally and personally, conducted long-running debates about the quantum realm that are now regarded as perhaps the historic high point of scientific argument.

Einstein was also highly sceptical of quantum mechanics' description of interactions between particles happening instantaneously over vast distances. With no known way that such particles could 'communicate' with each other, Einstein dubbed the supposed phenomenon as 'spooky action at a distance'. In a letter to Max Born in 1924 detailing several of his quantum concerns, Einstein wrote: 'I find the idea quite intolerable that an electron exposed to radiation should choose *of its own free will* not only its moment to jump off but also its direction.' He continued, 'In that case, I would rather be a cobbler, or even an employee in a gaming house, than a physicist.'

It was not that Einstein believed quantum mechanics was fundamentally incorrect. More exactly, he believed it to be incomplete. He had described his 1905 quanta paper as 'heuristic' and he considered quantum physics in much the same light. In 1926 he expressed his feelings to Max Born: 'Quantum mechanics is certainly imposing. But an inner voice tells me that this is not yet the real thing. The theory yields much, but it hardly brings us closer to the Old One's [God's] secrets.'

Even as the experimental data supporting the quantum cause grew, Einstein insisted that 'the last word has not been said'. Therefore he devoted a large part of his energies to challenging emerging quantum orthodoxies until the end of his life. Perversely, as each of his challenges was addressed, quantum mechanics was strengthened through the process of rigorous examination.

Einstein hoped that his 1935 EPR paper (co-authored with Boris Podolsky and Nathan Rosen and officially entitled 'Can Quantum Mechanical Description of Physical Reality Be Considered Complete?') would be the last nail in the coffin of quantum mechanics as it was then developing. It addressed one of his greatest objections, concerning the assertion that no single particle has a definite position until it is observed, an idea that had Einstein retorting: 'Do you really believe that the moon is not there unless we are looking at it?' The EPR paper expounded on a thought experiment that seemed to undermine the uncertainty principle, but it did not land the killer blow he had been expecting. It took a while, but in the 1980s his argument was at last experimentally disproven and the quantumites were destined for the last word, on this particular point at least.

In a 1944 exchange with Max Born, Einstein neatly summarized the essence of his conflict with the new branch of science: 'We have become Antipodean in our scientific expectations. You believe in the God who plays dice, and I in complete law and order in a world which objectively exists.' The great scientist was left clinging to what was, after all, an article of faith: that there is an objective reality. In 2005, John Polkinghorne, a British theoretical physicist and theologian, wrote in *Science and Theology News*:

Einstein wanted a physical world that was unproblematically objective and deterministic, hence his rejection of modern quantum theory. This stance made him the last of the great ancients, rather than the first of the moderns.

Think Even Bigger

'I'm still working passionately, though most of my intellectual offspring are ending up prematurely in the cemetery of disappointed hopes.'

ALBERT EINSTEIN, 1937

In part a response to his growing dissatisfaction with quantum theory, Einstein spent roughly the last thirty years of his life attempting to define what he termed a 'unified field theory'. Having fallen in love as a young man with the elegance of Maxwell's electromagnetic field, he now wanted to master the equations that would integrate the apparently incompatible elements of the electromagnetic and gravitational fields. Success in devising such a 'theory of everything', it was said, would be akin to reading God's mind.

One could not fault his ambition. In his 1923 Nobel lecture, 'Fundamental ideas and problems of the theory of relativity', he laid out his ambitions: 'A mathematically unified field theory is sought in which the gravitational field and the electromagnetic field are interpreted only as different components or manifestations of the same uniform field.'

Yet the quest was utterly out of kilter with the wider trends of science. Einstein desired theories straightforward enough that 'even a child could understand them'. In

1949 he wrote: 'A theory is more impressive the greater the simplicity of its premises, the more different things it relates, and the more expanded its area of applicability.' But this flew in the face of quantum developments. Einstein was attempting to impose all-embracing rules on the universe even as Bohr, Schrödinger and others were preaching a doctrine that rendered scientific principles less unified than ever.

Many in the quantum community believed Einstein's ambitions were rather outdated. There is swimming against the tide, and then there is trying to hold it back single-handed. Furthermore, he lacked the intuitive springboard upon which he had been able to rely in his earlier work. He was suddenly flailing, where previously he had known instinctively in which direction he should jump. The whole idea of the unified theory was really little more than a hunch.

Some regarded his pursuit of it as utter folly and a waste of his immense talents. It is often argued even today that his truly significant scientific contributions ended in 1935 with the EPR paper. Bohr came to regard him as little more than an alchemist, intent on discovering a scientific secret that simply didn't exist, and Schrödinger called him a fool for persevering.

But it is not quite fair to characterize him as a dolt in his dotage, obsessively pursuing a fool's errand. Einstein correctly believed that if he successfully formulated a unified field theory, it would outstrip all of his previous achievements. But he also understood that it might be beyond even him – as he would comment in 1934:'I have locked myself into quite hopeless scientific problems.' Nonetheless, he felt a duty to try, not least because the general theory had brought him the financial and professional freedom to do so. 'I no longer need to take part in the competition of the big brains,' he once said to Paul Ehrenfest. He was in a rare position to take a risk that others could not.

In this light, his work on a theory of everything was enormously courageous. The 'anxious searching in the dark' certainly took its toll, the quest being the most frustrating of his life, as this section's introductory quote illustrates. In 1951, he told Maurice Solovine that the unified field theory 'has been put into retirement', but it never was. Having succeeded with the general theory, Einstein's extraordinary intellectual ambition forced him to push himself to his very limits. It was as if Christopher Columbus decided to trump his discovery of the New World by trying to sail to a previously undiscovered planet. The ambition is to be admired, and failure to achieve the goal should not detract from the brilliance of his earlier achievements.

But Einstein's hunt came at a cost. In old age, he was an increasingly isolated figure within the scientific community. He paid the price for his suspicion that quantum theory was on the wrong track – a suspicion that time has shown was misplaced. And yet, today, although there is little serious appetite for a unified field theory as Einstein saw it, a good deal of the work he produced in its pursuit has been integrated into modern string theory, the scientific field that seems to offer us the greatest hopes of bringing together the Einsteinian and quantum universes.

On 25 May 1953, Einstein wrote a letter, the words of which reveal the rationale behind his decision to pursue the apparently unobtainable: 'Every individual … has to retain his way of thinking if he does not want to get lost in the maze of possibilities.' It also illuminates a man familiar with self-doubt: 'However, nobody is sure of having taken the right road, me the least.'

That is the price of thinking *really* big.

Be a Political Animal

'My passionate interest in social justice and social responsibility has always stood in curious contrast to a marked lack of desire for direct association with men and women.'

ALBERT EINSTEIN, 1932

Einstein had a well-defined political consciousness from early childhood, as evidenced by his refusal to rush after his classmates to watch the military processions that rolled past his Munich school. The fame that came his way, in particular from 1919 onwards, gave him the platform from which he could bring his world view to bear. Almost mirroring the waning of his influence among his scientific contemporaries, he became a giant of global politics.

This did not necessarily sit easily with him, since he regarded politics as necessarily temporary but science as timeless. 'Politics is for the present,' he said, 'while our equations are for eternity.' Nonetheless, amid the political turmoil of the first half of the twentieth century, he felt morally compelled to speak out time and again. He expanded on his motivation to do so in a 1927 interview with *Neue Zürcher Zeitung*:

Of course I am not a politician in the conventional sense of the word; few scholars are. At the same time, I believe that no one should shirk the political task …

of restoring the unity between nations that has been completely destroyed by the world war and seeing to it that a better and more genuine understanding among nations makes it impossible to repeat the dreadful catastrophe we have lived through.

Underpinning his beliefs were the twin pillars of social justice and individual freedom ('Striving for social justice is the most valuable thing to do in life,' he claimed in 1934). As with his scientific endeavours, he would change and adapt his position to take account of fresh developments as they happened. We shall see the rise of Hitler was one such occurrence that prompted him to significantly adjust his principles.

He honed his generally liberal outlook in youth with the likes of Jost Winteler in Aarau and counted among his friends at Zurich Polytechnic Gustav Maier – a Jewish banker and founder of the Swiss branch of the Society for Ethical Culture – and Friedrich Adler, son of the leader of the Austrian Social Democratic Party. (Adler would go on to shoot dead the Minister-President of Austria-Hungary, Count Karl von Stürgkh, in a politically motivated murder in 1916.)

By nature a pacifist with a distrust of over-powerful nation states, Einstein had broad (but not unequivocal) socialist sympathies. In 1952 he would proclaim Mahatma Gandhi as 'the greatest political genius of our time'. Always at the centre of Einstein's ethos were the rights of the individual, which he considered integral to the wider social good. At a speech at London's Royal Albert Hall in 1933, he stated: 'Only in a free society is man able to create the inventions and cultural values which make life worthwhile to modern man.' Nineteen years later, his view had not changed:

It is important for the common good to foster individuality: for only the individual can produce the new ideas which the community needs for its continuous improvement and requirements – indeed, to avoid sterility and petrification.

Unsurprisingly, then, he was a staunch defender of civil rights, too, a position that sometimes brought him into conflict with some of his fellow citizens after his move to the USA. He was an outspoken critic of racism, telling the *Cheyney Record* – a student paper from a black college in Pennsylvania – in 1948:

Race prejudice is a part of a tradition which – conditioned by history – is uncritically handed down from one generation to another. The only remedy is enlightenment and education. This is a slow and painstaking process in which all right-thinking people should take part.

He had caused something of a furore eleven years earlier when he hosted the black singer, Marian Anderson, at his home after a local inn had refused her a room when she came to Princeton for a concert. It was the start of a friendship that saw him welcome her to his home on Mercer Street several times over the ensuing years and sent out a powerful message. He also publicly backed the cause of the Scottsboro Boys (nine black teenagers accused of rape in Alabama in the early 1930s), whose convictions before all-white juries are widely considered miscarriages of justice. Furthermore, he enthusiastically advocated for Tom Mooney, a white labour activist who served twenty-two years in prison for allegedly perpetrating a bombing in San Francisco in 1916 before finally receiving a pardon in 1939.

Despite his impassioned interest in the affairs of man, Einstein nevertheless always felt more at home immersed in the natural sciences rather than the political ones. Once asked in the post-nuclear bomb age why it had been easier to discover atoms than it had been to control their use, he replied, 'This is simple, my friend: because politics is more difficult than physics.'

Be a Citizen
of the World

'I am by heritage a Jew, by citizenship a Swiss, and by
disposition a human being, and *only* a human being,
without any special attachment to any state
or national entity whatsoever.'

ALBERT EINSTEIN, 1918

One of the most radical aspects of Einstein's politics was his refutation of the ascendancy of the nation state in an age where few challenged its pre-eminence. The deep irony was that in the face of his staunch opposition, he became a citizen of far more countries than the average person – Germany, Switzerland, Austria-Hungary and the USA (though not Israel, despite being offered the chance to be its president).

Beginning while he was still alive and continuing in analyses of his legacy, it has often been said that Einstein was politically naïve. It is true that he was perhaps sometimes easily 'signed up' to one cause or another, blunting his incisiveness as a political commentator and occasionally allying him with characters not really worthy of the honour, but his politics was sharper than is often credited.

Some have argued that his repudiation of the nation state was an overly simplistic position. However, given that global geopolitics over his lifetime was dominated by two world wars, both of which had their origins in nationalist aggression, it is quite possible to follow the logic behind his view. Moreover, it was not one he adopted retrospectively, but was something he believed from a very young age. His rejection of Germany's streak of Prussian militarism saw him renounce his German nationality at an age where most of his contemporaries were revising for their exams or worrying about an outbreak of acne. As he entered adulthood, Einstein was stateless by his own hand.

He realized that the global overthrow of the nation state system was not feasible, although in his ideal world that would have been the case (in 1929 he told the one-time President of Baden in Germany: 'If we did not have to live among intolerant, narrow-minded and violent people, I would be the first to discard all nationalism in favour of a universal humanity.'). That being the case, he longed for a reconfiguration of nationhood in favour of his common theme, the individual. In an article entitled 'The Road to Peace', published in *The New York Times Magazine* in 1931, he argued:

> The State exists for man, not man for the State ... I believe that the most important mission of the State is to protect the individual and make it possible for him to develop into a creative personality. The State should be our servant; we should not be slaves of the State.

Although his scepticism of nationalism was well established by the time of the outbreak of the First World

War, the rise of Hitler saw him make the argument in public with renewed passion. 'Nationalism is an infantile disease, the measles of mankind,' he told a newspaper interviewer in 1929. Four years later, in front of a London audience, he said: 'Nationalism is, in my opinion, nothing more than an idealistic rationalization for militarism and aggression.'

He swore his US citizenship in 1940, having turned down the opportunity to be fast-tracked five years earlier by the passage of a special congressional bill designed for him personally. In the same year, the FBI had informed President Roosevelt that Einstein was not suitable for employment on projects of a 'secret nature' as 'it seems unlikely that a man of his background could, in such a short time, become a loyal American citizen'. It was an unfounded slur, but to his dying day Einstein had scant concern with being an accepted member of any national club. *The New York Times* quoted him in 1926 thus:

> Why do people speak of great men in terms of nationality? Great Germans, great Englishmen? Goethe always protested against being called a German poet. Great men are simply men and are not to be considered from the point of view of nationality, nor should the environment in which they were brought up be taken into account.

Einstein and Pacifism

'The psychological roots of war are, in my opinion,
biologically rooted in the aggressive nature
of the male creature …'

ALBERT EINSTEIN IN 'MY OPINION
OF THE WAR', 1915

As modern warfare made possible slaughter on an industrial scale, Einstein became one of the most famous advocates of pacifism in the world. However, the excesses of the Hitler regime led him to tweak his doctrine.

We have already detailed Einstein's anti-militarist leanings, which he had nurtured from childhood. These were reflected in adulthood as he was able to avoid enforced military service after surrendering his German citizenship in 1896 and was then overlooked for Swiss military service thanks to a combination of foot ailments and varicose veins. Utterly opposed to the concept of such enforced training (he regarded it as akin to state-imposed slavery), he was presumably not too distraught that his health had let him down in this way.

The First World War and the resulting decimation of his generation sparked Einstein into increasingly strong advocations of pacifism. 'At times such as this,' he said as the war started in 1914, 'one realizes what a sorry species one belongs to.' This was the culmination of something he had long feared: Europe 'in its madness' embarking 'on something incredibly preposterous'.

What came as more of a shock to him was the willingness of so many of his scientific colleagues, many of whom he deeply admired, to pin their colours to the mast of war. If it came as little surprise that Philipp Lenard was among the pro-war lobby, the presence of several others was a significant disappointment to Einstein. For example, Fritz Haber – the 1918 Nobel Chemistry Laureate – was key to the development of chemical weapons and oversaw the German attack at Ypres in April 1915 that claimed 5,000 French and Belgian lives. Walther Nernst, who would win the Nobel Chemistry Prize in 1920, was similarly involved in the development of chemical weapons.

But perhaps most appalling of all for Einstein was Max Planck's public declaration that the war was a just one. Haber, Nernst and Planck were all signatories to the so-called Manifesto of the Ninety-Three (also known rather darkly as the 'Appeal to the Cultured World'), a petition issued in October 1914 that defended Germany's conduct and proclaimed the necessity of the war. Einstein responded by lending his name to an alternative petition, a 'Manifesto to Europeans' – the brainchild of the physician and founder of the intellectualist New Fatherland League, Georg Nicolai (also a friend of Elsa Einstein). It called for an end to aggressive nationalism but went unpublished after failing to secure a groundswell of support.

Nonetheless, Einstein continued to use his public profile to call for a quick end to the war and to propose a federalist Europe. In November 1915, he composed an essay, 'My Opinion of the War', that blamed the sexual character of the male for the aggression that brought about wars. He also promoted the idea of an international organization charged with policing nation states. It was a concept he would develop and expand upon until his death. In 1935, for instance, he said in an interview with *Survey Graphic*:

National loyalty is limiting; men must be taught to think in world terms. Every country will have to surrender a portion of its sovereignty through international cooperation. To avoid destruction, aggression must be sacrificed.

In the 1920s, against the backdrop of rising Nazism in Germany, his advocacy of pacifism strengthened and he played an active role in several peace campaigns. At the time, this seemed to him one of few viable routes to mediate against what he described as the world's apparent failure 'to fear even the most extreme and catastrophic inhumanity and murderousness of war'. In 1922, he joined the League of Nations Committee on Intellectual Cooperation, a body founded to promote cross-border cultural and intellectual exchange in the interests of world peace.

Like his greatest scientific endeavours, his political commitment to pacifism was a leap of faith based on 'an instinctive feeling'; one he said had overwhelmed him 'because the murder of men is disgusting'. In 1929, he achieved the considerable feat of upsetting both the German militaristic right and those who believed armed confrontation was the only way to counter its rise. Einstein declared: 'I would unconditionally refuse all war service, direct or indirect regardless of how I might feel about the causes of any particular war.'

By 1931 he was describing himself as a 'militant pacifist', convinced that the only way to end war was for people themselves to refuse to fight. But Hitler's ascent from vitriolic extremist to German Chancellor in 1933 changed things, prompting Einstein to reassess his views. It is true that he remained passionately behind the notion of pacifism, as when he explained to a United Nations radio interviewer in 1950:

> I believe that Gandhi's views were the most enlightened among all of the political men of our time. We should strive to do things in his spirit; not to use violence in fighting for our cause, but by non-participation in what we believe is evil.

But as Hitler imposed his state apparatus of fear once in office – directing it with particular ferocity against the Jewish population – Einstein acknowledged that there were circumstances in which pacifism was insufficient. In 1954 he explained to the writer, H. Herbert Fox, how he adapted his outlook:

> I have always been a pacifist, i.e., I have declined to recognize brute force as a means for the solution of international conflicts. Nevertheless, it is, in my

opinion, not reasonable to cling to that principle unconditionally. An exception has necessarily to be made if a hostile power threatens wholesale destruction of one's own group.

In the face of Hitlerism, he argued that military service could be undertaken 'in the knowledge of serving European civilization', and in 1948 he told members of the War Resisters' League (set up in the early 1920s as a response to the First World War) that refusal to take part in military activities was 'too primitive' an approach to adopt universally.

The treatment of the Jews was a crime for which Einstein could never forgive Germany. He had surrendered his citizenship for a second time in 1933 and, eleven years later, commented on the slaughter in the Warsaw ghetto and the deaths of upwards of 300,000 people accordingly: 'The Germans, as a whole nation, are responsible for these mass killings and should be punished as a people.'

A year later, his stance had not softened as he discussed with his German friend (and the 1925 Nobel Physics Laureate) James Franck his view that Germany had murdered millions of civilians according to a well-prepared plan. 'They would do it all again if only they were able to,' he suggested. 'Not a trace of guilt or remorse is to be found among them.' Having had his works subjected to the Nazi book burnings, Einstein took his own small revenge in the post-war years by putting an embargo on publication of his books in Germany.

The shock of the world wars left him with an understandably downbeat view of humanity's prospects. 'As long as there is man, there will be war,' he asserted in 1947. He was convinced more than ever that the nation state system needed a thorough overhaul if there was to be any hope. His vision was of a supranational organization with real teeth – one, as he would put it in the same year, 'with sufficient legislative and executive powers to keep the peace'. It should, in effect, act as an international police force, applying as required the judgements of an international court of arbitration. That is to say, a power to which individual countries answered rather than the other way round. To his disappointment, neither the League of Nations (created in the aftermath of the First World War) or the United Nations (established after the Second World War) was given the muscle to succeed in this aim. Given the history of compromises that has seen the UN too often accused of subservience to one national power or another, his fears were not without foundation.

Though well intentioned, Einstein's commitment to a global federalist organization left him open to accusations of hopeless idealism. That is a claim not without basis. However, he was an individual who had seen the dangers of nationalism at first hand and knew better than most how the stakes had been upped in the nuclear age. In his view, hopelessness lay in rejection of global federalism. As he told journalists shortly after the end of the Second World War: 'The only salvation for civilization and the human race lies in the creation of world governance.'

Einstein and Fascism

'As long as I have any choice in the matter, I shall
live only in a country where civil liberty, tolerance
and equality of all citizens before the law prevail.
These conditions do not exist in Germany
at the present time.'

ALBERT EINSTEIN, 1933

As a left-leaning liberal democrat living in Germany – and a Jew with a global profile – Einstein was on an inevitable collision course with Hitler. The Nazi regime was the epitome of everything that Einstein feared would spring from the German traditions of nationalism and militarism that he so distrusted. In particular, he despised the anti-intellectualism of the right. In 1930, he contributed an essay, 'Science and Dictatorship', to a book entitled *Dictatorship on Trial*. In it, he wrote: 'A dictatorship means muzzles all round, and consequently stultification. Science can flourish only in an atmosphere of free speech.' Nonetheless, Hitler's meteoric rise took him by surprise.

Even as late as 1931, Einstein seems to have believed that Hitler was working on borrowed time, able to make political capital only as a result of the economic mess that grew out of the ferocity of the post-First World War Versailles Treaty, hyperinflation and mass unemployment. 'He is living – or shall I say sitting – on the empty stomach of Germany,' he argued. 'As soon as economic conditions improve, he will no longer be important.' Retrospectively, his words can be recycled to support the suggestion of political naïvety, but then there were far more seasoned politicians who continued to underestimate Hitler.

By the time the Nazi leader had been anointed Chancellor, Einstein harboured few, if any, illusions about the nature of the beast. He would write in 1935: 'Hitler appeared, a man with limited intellectual abilities and unfit for any useful work, bursting with envy and bitterness against all whom circumstance and nature had favoured over him.' Within months of Hitler becoming Chancellor at the beginning of 1933, Einstein was asking: 'Doesn't the world see that Hitler is aiming for war?'

Einstein being among the most famous German Jews in the world, he was singled out for particular attention by the Nazi party. There was said to be a bounty on his head and in a National Socialist publication listing 'enemies of the state' there appeared a photo of Einstein, cold-bloodedly captioned 'Not yet hanged'. When Einstein and Elsa left for what should have been a temporary sojourn to the USA at the end of 1932, they did not know that they would never return to Germany. However, as the couple left their beloved home at Caputh, a few miles south of Potsdam, he is supposed to have turned to her and said: 'Take a very good look at it. You will never see it again.' Sure enough, within weeks of Hitler coming to power, their residence at Caputh was raided. In due course, the Nazi administration confiscated both the property and Einstein's boat, which was kept on the grounds.

Einstein went on the offensive, starting with the renunciation of his citizenship and his resignation from the Prussian Academy of Sciences (before he could be cast out on the grounds of his Jewishness). Speaking in London later in the year, he attacked the barbarism of the German regime, saying: 'If we want to resist the powers that threaten to suppress intellectual and individual freedom, we must be clear what is at stake.' Without such freedoms, he argued, 'there would have been no Shakespeare, no Goethe, no Newton, no Faraday, no Pasteur, no Lister'.

He became convinced that Germany, drilled for centuries in 'slavish submission, military routine and brutality', would not step back from the brink. Turning his back on his pacifist code for the time being, he argued that other European nations had no choice but to prepare a military response, it being a lesser evil to prevent a greater one. As Europe's diplomats practised appeasement in their ill-fated pursuit of peace, Einstein was ironically one of the most prominent voices calling for force to be used against Hitler, almost from the moment he came to power. It is a grim reflection of the politics of the age that in 1938 – just a year before war broke out – the latest student intake at Princeton voted Einstein only second in a poll of the greatest living people – a place behind Hitler.

The rise of Nazism and the onset of the Second World War served as proof that Einstein's long-held fears of nationalism and authoritarianism were well placed.

Einstein and Fascism

The failure of the German intelligentsia to stand up to Hitler (indeed, many of his erstwhile colleagues actively collaborated with and supported the regime) would haunt him for the rest of his life. As the old aphorism had it, evil prevails when good men do nothing.

Having been forced from the land of his birth, he had found a new home in the USA – a country that could delight and infuriate him in equal measure. When Senator Joe McCarthy embarked on his infamous anti-communist witch hunt in the 1950s, Einstein felt compelled to speak out against what he perceived as another attack by a state on individual freedom. He advised a New York teacher, William Frauenglass, who had been called before a committee investigating 'un-American activities', that he should not cooperate. He reasoned that it was 'shameful for a blameless citizen to submit to such an inquisition'.

McCarthy responded that anyone telling Americans to 'keep secret information which they may have about spies and saboteurs is himself an enemy of America'. Elements of the press meanwhile depicted Einstein as ungrateful and conspiring with the enemy. A lifelong campaigner for liberty, he thus found himself living in the land of the free but, just as ever, as an outsider treated with suspicion.

Einstein and Socialism

'I have never been a communist. But if I were,
I would not be ashamed of it.'

ALBERT EINSTEIN, 1950

In an era of paranoia over 'Reds under the beds', Einstein was regularly required to defend himself against allegations that he was an apologist for the worst excesses of Stalin. Though his enemies resorted to crude character assassination, it was his nuanced relationship with socialism that undoubtedly caused the smoke for the fire, and is worth a closer examination.

Einstein felt an identification with socialist politics and economics, and harboured grave doubts about the ability of unfettered capitalism to meet the world's needs. In 1945 he critiqued capitalism in an essay called 'Is there room for individual freedom in a Socialist State?':

What is a capitalist state? It is a state in which the principal means of production, such as farmland, real estate in the cities, the supply of water, gas, and electricity, public transportation, as well as the larger industrial plants are owned by a minority of the citizenry. Productivity is geared toward making a profit for the owners rather than providing the population with a uniform distribution of essential goods ...

Back in 1932, he had written that he was convinced 'no amount of wealth can help humanity forward, even in the hands of the most dedicated worker in this cause'. Fifteen years later, he was, perhaps against expectation, talking about technological progress in terms of its threat to employment. Einstein wanted the dissolution of class difference, and socialism offered up this prospect. Yet so did that bastion of capitalism, America, where, as Einstein put it, 'no one humbles himself before another person or class'.

His sympathy for socialism, however, was always secondary to his support for individual liberty. Viewing everything through that prism, his attitude to socialism, and especially to the form it took in Russia, was far more complex than was often understood. He was by no stretch of the imagination an acolyte of Moscow. Even as the Bolsheviks were seizing power in 1917, he was urging: 'All true democrats must stand guard lest the old class tyranny of the right be replaced by a new class tyranny of the left.'

He never visited Russia for fear that his presence might be hijacked for propaganda purposes, and in 1933 he declared himself an adversary of Bolshevism as much as fascism, or any other dictatorship, for that matter. That said, there were some misjudgements along the way. In the mid-1930s he turned down the opportunity to sign a petition protesting Stalin's murderous approach to dealing with his rivals. Instead, he spoke of regret that the USSR's leaders had 'let themselves be carried away', before asserting: 'The Russians have proved that their only aim is really the improvement of the lot of the Russian people.'

He was, in his own words, 'not blind to the serious weakness of the Russian system of government', but felt it had 'great merits' and doubted whether 'softer methods' would have allowed for its survival. Nonetheless, he recoiled at the 'complete repression' of the individual and freedom of speech, and decried 'power-hungry individuals' employing foul means to further their own ends. There was clearly a conflict between his attraction to the underlying ideology and his rejection of the state machinery used to impose it. It should also be emphasized that he was by no means the only intellectual of the period to give the Kremlin the occasional benefit of the doubt.

Einstein's reward for his perceived equivocation was attacks from all sides. Moscow regarded him with suspicion, with some interpreting his urgings for a supranational government as part of a capitalist conspiracy. And while the US public loved Einstein, the government was always more wary. The FBI, for instance, assembled a dossier on him that ran to just short of 1,500 pages (yet still failed to pick up on his affair from 1941 until 1945 with Margarita Konenkova, a Greenwich Village stalwart and Soviet spy – a fact of which Einstein was himself apparently oblivious).

His anti-McCarthy stance did little to take the heat off, as when he said in 1954: 'America is incomparably less endangered by its own communists than by the hysterical hunt for the few communists who are here.' He was simply being a realist on the question. If the western European nations were not paranoid about a communist takeover, he reasoned, why should the USA be? Especially when that paranoia endangered the US's greatest attribute, its reverence for personal liberty.

Einstein was a socialist, then, insofar as the philosophy advocated social equality. But, above anything else, he was always a libertarian.

Consider the Moral Implications of Your Work

'The great scientist of our age, he was truly a seeker after truth who would not compromise with evil or untruth.'

JAWAHARLAL NEHRU, INDEPENDENT INDIA'S FIRST PRIME MINISTER, 1955

Einstein is one of those rare figures who achieved greatness in two disparate fields – namely, theoretical physics and humanitarianism. For long periods of his life, he clung to the belief that these areas could be kept apart. Science enlivened him while politics, like personal relationships, tired him, so it is little wonder that he should wish to keep his scientific work 'sacred' and unsullied. However, as he saw his own scientific breakthroughs hijacked for the most grotesque of political ends – the creation and unregulated proliferation of the atomic bomb – he understood (albeit reluctantly) that these two parts of his life were eventually colliding.

There is a naïve charm to his statement, made in 1923, that 'it is not right to bring politics into scientific matters'. It was a sentiment he attempted to cling to, long after he had been forced to accept that such a separation was artificial. Even in 1949, for instance, he was still suggesting that his 'love for justice and the striving to contribute toward the improvement of human conditions are quite independent from my scientific interests'.

The realist in Einstein, however, had long

acknowledged that science was failing in what should have been its underlying aim: to improve the human condition. Instead, he saw around him a world where scientific and technological development had 'enslaved men to machines' and allowed them to 'poison and mutilate one another' in war, while making peacetime 'hurried and uncertain'. These were views he held even before he had considered that his science might be harnessed for the creation of the atomic bomb – the weapon that compelled Einstein to accept that scientific work could not be undertaken without reference to its effects (predicted and unforeseen) upon the wider world. In 1948 he was quoted in *The New York Times* as saying:

> We scientists, whose tragic destiny it has been to help make the methods of annihilation ever more gruesome and more effective, must consider it our solemn and transcendent duty to do all in our power to prevent these weapons from being used for the brutal purpose for which they were invented.

Contrary to his will, science and morality had thus become entwined. In a private letter written to a New York vicar a couple of years later, Einstein explained: 'The most important human endeavour is the striving for morality in our actions. Our inner balance and even our very existence depend on it.' While he may have missed the separation between Einstein the man of physics and Einstein the global humanitarian, it was the melding of these personalities that marked him out for greatness. In the words of the great British writer and chemist, C. P. Snow:

To me, he appears as out of comparison the greatest intellect of this century, and almost certainly the greatest personification of moral experience. He was in many ways different from the rest of the species.

EINSTEIN AND THE BOMB

'Science has brought forth this danger, but the real problem is in the minds and hearts of men.'

ALBERT EINSTEIN IN INTERVIEW WITH MICHAEL AMRINE, *THE NEW YORK TIMES MAGAZINE*, 1946

It was Einstein's cruel fate that history would forge an eternal association between him and the mushroom cloud of the nuclear bomb. The tale of his involvement in the creation of the weapon and his subsequent battle for arms control serves as a sort of modern fable.

The invention of the bomb is rooted in Einstein's most famous equation: $E=mc^2$. If the nucleus of the atom could be split, it would be possible to release huge amounts of (potentially destructive) energy. In 1938, news reached Einstein that Otto Hahn and Fritz Strassmann in Berlin had succeeded in doing just that. It was an achievement that Einstein had considered all but impossible just three years before, when he had suggested it was 'akin to shooting birds in the dark in a place where there are only a few birds'. But even as he reflected on the development in his office in Princeton, he was not overly concerned.

Then in the summer of 1939, as the Second World War was starting, he received a visit from an old Hungarian colleague, Leó Szilárd. Szilárd had been working on uranium fission and realized it could be used to create a weapon of unimagined destruction. His fear was that Germany might start buying up the vast uranium supplies available in the Belgian Congo. He hoped that Einstein might be able to bring his influence with the Belgian royal family to bear. However, before long it was decided that in fact it would be more pertinent to send a warning letter to the US President, Franklin D. Roosevelt. The letter – dated 2 August 1939, drafted by Szilárd and signed by Einstein – began:

Some recent work by E. Fermi and L. Szilárd, which has been communicated to me in manuscript, leads me to expect that the element uranium may be turned into a new and important source of energy in the immediate future. Certain aspects of the situation which has arisen seem to call for watchfulness and, if necessary, quick action on the part of the administration.

It would go on to warn ominously of 'extremely powerful bombs of a new type', and continued:

In view of this situation you may think it desirable to have some permanent contact maintained between the administration and the group of physicists working on chain reactions in America.

The key chain reaction was the one set off by this letter. At first the Roosevelt administration dithered but, after further correspondence with Einstein, the Manhattan Project was established in late 1941. Under the guidance of J. Robert Oppenheimer, it would result in the creation of the atom bomb, which was employed twice before the end of the Second World War.

Einstein himself had no involvement in the project, bar some secondary research that was eventually integrated. Indeed, he was not even officially told that the Manhattan Project existed, J. Edgar Hoover's FBI having assembled an error-strewn report that deemed him a security risk. Even if they had not, though, it is unlikely Einstein would have wanted direct involvement in an enterprise so contrary to his core principles. 'My scientific work has no more than a very indirect connection to the atomic bomb,' he assured Hans Albert in a letter in 1945.

However, by 1944 he was aware that the bomb was close to completion. Convinced that the authorities lacked a firm grasp of the implications, he renewed his calls for a supranational body and urged his fellow scientists to campaign for an 'internationalization of military power'. When his secretary, Helen Dukas, broke the news to him on 6 August 1945 that the USA had dropped the bomb on the Japanese city of Hiroshima, his only words were, 'Oh, my God.' A second city, Nagasaki, would be bombed a few days later.

In the immediate aftermath, Einstein emerged as one of the foremost voices pleading for international cooperation to mitigate against the new dangers the world now faced. Before the year was out, he made one of the greatest speeches of his life, at the Fifth Nobel Anniversary Dinner at the Hotel Astor in New York. He began by drawing a parallel between the physicists who had worked on the bomb and Alfred Nobel, who instigated the eponymous prizes in part to relieve his conscience, having created a powerful explosive of his own. He went on to paint a grim picture of the delicate global balance:

The war is won, but the peace is not. The great powers, united in fighting, are now divided over the peace settlements. The world was promised freedom from fear, but in fact fear has increased tremendously since the termination of the war ...

Einstein most certainly felt guilt for his own part in the weapon's creation. Speaking in November 1954, he said, 'I made one great mistake in my life – when I signed that letter to President Roosevelt recommending that atom bombs be made ...' But hindsight is a wonderful thing, and the implications of Hitler getting the bomb first were unthinkable. In fact, Germany was hamstrung in its quest almost from the outset. This was largely the result of its own anti-Semitic legislation that had forced some fourteen Nobel laureates and almost half the country's professors of theoretical physics into exile. 'Had I known that the Germans would not succeed in producing an atomic bomb,' Einstein told *Newsweek* magazine in 1947, 'I never would have lifted a finger.'

He was relentless in his warnings against complacency. 'As long as sovereign states continue to have armaments and armaments secrets, new world wars will be inevitable,' he told a press conference in 1945. A letter he wrote to the Emergency Committee of Atomic Scientists

(ECAS) in 1946 said: 'The unleashed power of the atom bomb has changed everything except our modes of thinking, and thus we drift toward unparalleled catastrophes.' Einstein had co-founded ECAS specifically to promote world peace and the peaceful use of nuclear energy.

He lacked faith in the ability of the recently inaugurated United Nations to keep its members in check and was a vociferous opponent of unilateral disarmament, a policy he was convinced would benefit only those intent on arming. The spectre of Cold War rivalries only added to the gloom. In February 1951 he was interviewed on NBC's *Today with Mrs. Roosevelt* (hosted by the former First Lady) about the arms race. 'Each step appears as the inevitable consequence of the one that went before,' he said. 'And at the end, looming ever clearer, lies general annihilation.'

Yet his pessimism never grew so great that it entirely overran his sense of hope. A few days before his death, he signed what became known as the Russell–Einstein Manifesto. It was the brainchild of the British mathematician and philosopher Bertrand Russell, and highlighted the dangers the world faced in the nuclear age. It became the founding document of the Pugwash Conferences, established two years later for academics and public figures to consider the most pressing questions of global security, and is perhaps most memorable for a single phrase: 'Remember your humanity, and forget the rest.'

Russell was a great admirer of Einstein, and looked back on his life in a broadcast ten years later:

Einstein was not only a great scientist, he was a great man. He stood for peace in a world drifting towards war. He remained sane in a mad world, and liberal in a world of fanatics.

Make Celebrity Work for You

'Everyone should be respected as an individual,
but no one idolized.'

ALBERT EINSTEIN, 1930

As Einstein worked away on his 1905 papers in between his chores at the patent office, it is safe to assume that he was not doing it for the fame and the glory. Even after publishing his general theory of relativity, he was hardly a household name, even if he was an acknowledged star in the scientific fraternity.

But with news of Eddington's light deflection results in 1919, Einstein was thrust into the glare of the global spotlight. The following year he would speak to his old friend Heinrich Zangger of the cult that had built up around him, which made him feel like a 'pagan idol'. 'But this, too, God willing, will pass,' he wrote over-optimistically. That year he would also confide in Hendrik Lorentz that he was more aware than ever of his limitations, arguing that his 'faculties have been quite overrated'. He described the gap he perceived between his achievements and the popular estimate of them as 'simply grotesque'. By 1921, his weariness with fame was evident in a quote in the socialist daily, *New York Call*: 'I do not care to speak about my work. The sculptor, the artist, the musician, the scientist work because they love their work. Fame and honour are secondary.'

It is true, too, that by and large he did not seek out the trappings of fame and fortune. 'Possessions, outward success, publicity, luxury – to me these have always been contemptible. I believe that a simple and unassuming life is best for … the body and mind,' he wrote in 'What I Believe' in 1930. The year before, he had spoken of the unfairness, and even bad taste, inherent in society's selection of a few individuals for boundless admiration. Materially, he lived a decent life, spending significant sums, for instance, on his home in Caputh and on his passion for sailing. But excess was not for him. His Princeton home on Mercer Street was noted for being strikingly 'normal', and in old age he was renowned for giving his time to help local children with their homework. He rarely played at being the great celebrity.

He also managed to maintain a healthy streak of scepticism about the nature of fame. Amid the first flush of his celebrity in 1919, he wrote in *The Times*:

> By an application of the theory of relativity to the taste
> of readers, today in Germany I am called a German
> man of science, and in England I am represented as a
> Swiss Jew. If I come to be represented as a *bête noire*,
> the descriptions will be reversed, and I shall become
> a Swiss Jew for the Germans and a German man of
> science for the English!

On another occasion, he acerbically whispered to a companion during a particularly long address during a National Academy of Sciences dinner in his honour: 'I have just got a new theory of eternity.' And in an interview with *The New York Times* in 1944, he posed the existential question: 'Why is it that nobody understands me, yet everybody likes me?'

However, it would be false to suggest he abhorred his celebrity. In 1920, for example, he was happy to cooperate with Alexander Moszkowski on a biography. He clearly enjoyed the company of certain famous people, too, as when he pursued a meeting with Charlie Chaplin. While accusations that he practised self-promotion were often politically charged, even allies like C. P. Snow would suggest that a part of him revelled in the attention. Put simply, it is unlikely you will appear on the cover of *Time* magazine five times if you're an utter recluse. Whether consciously or not, he gave a good sound bite and was a capable performer in public life. Even his carefree approach to style ultimately added to the mystique, as we shall soon see.

It should be to his credit that he learned quickly how to utilize his fame after it was so unexpectedly thrust upon him. This was not a man, after all, who had been media trained in the manner that every sports star or pop idol is today. But he would in time make fine use of the platform that was available to him, exploiting it to spread a message of peace and international cooperation.

Even so, fame no doubt left him slightly bewildered.

He pondered: 'Why popular fancy should seize on me, a scientist, dealing in abstract things and happy if left alone, is a manifestation of mass psychology that is beyond me.'

Get the 'Mad Professor' Look

'The professor never wears socks. Even when he was invited by Mr Roosevelt to the White House he didn't wear socks.'

HELEN DUKAS

C ould you pick out Isaac Newton, Charles Darwin or Marie Curie in an identity parade? For most people, the answer is likely 'no'. But ask the same question regarding Einstein and a great many of us could give it a pretty good shot. That is because he was not only the most immediately recognizable scientist of his age, but of all time. A huge celebrity almost despite himself, his shock of hair, the bushy moustache, the hangdog eyes and the über-casual styling made him identifiable around the globe. Indeed, to this day the look is integral to the Einstein 'brand' – the epitome of unbounded genius.

Yet, the unkempt appearance was not always so. For the early part of his adult life, Einstein was quite the head-turner and in his student days attracted many women with his looks. His hair was richly dark and wavy, sitting atop a high forehead – all the better for storing that genius grey matter. Those penetrating brown eyes, so appealingly doleful when set in the wrinkled face of his later years, spoke more of an intense, inherent sorrowfulness in his younger years. They seemed utter proof of the old adage that the eyes are the windows to the soul.

He had a distinguished aquiline nose and a mouth that might best be described as sensuous. He was generally softly spoken, but when something amused him he would unleash a booming laugh not dissimilar to the barking of a seal. Archive photos show a striking, well-built fellow with a penchant for smart suits. He was undeniably debonair. Coupled with self-confidence, a sharp sense of humour and a streak of sarcasm that he retained all his life, it was inevitable that he would set many a heart aflutter. He was, in modern parlance, noted 'eye candy'.

However, it was not long before his characteristic quirkiness started to show itself. By nature, he had a relaxed attitude to clothes and was often to be observed wearing outfits that had seen better days. According to Abraham Pais, one of his biographers, Einstein once noted that, 'I like neither new clothes nor new kinds of food.' By the time he got his junior professorship in 1909, he was starting to adopt the dishevelled styling that became so famous.

Among his peculiarities was a refusal to wear socks, a propensity confirmed in the quote at the beginning of this section by his dedicated personal secretary, Helen Dukas. This was because, according to Einstein himself, when he was young he found that his big toes kept making holes in his socks, until he came to the decision that he would simply stop wearing them. The dapper suits eventually went as well, to be replaced by a distinctive uniform of baggy corduroy trousers, equally baggy sweatshirts (mostly cotton, thanks to a mild allergy to wool) and, very often, a leather jacket (an item of apparel that appealed for being hard-wearing and requiring little upkeep). To complete the look, a pair of slippers were commonly to be found on his sockless feet.

His commitment to sartorial informality became the stuff of legend. In 1932, as he was about to receive a delegation from Germany's President Paul von Hindenburg, Einstein's wife, Elsa, urged him to dress for the occasion. But he was having none of it. 'If they want to see me,' he said, 'here I am. If they want to see my clothes, open my closet.'

On another occasion, he is said to have responded to a suggestion that he dress more suitably for a trip to his office by saying: 'Why should I? Everyone knows me there.' But when told to reconsider his clothing for a conference he was attending, he argued: 'Why should I? No one knows me there.' Although he was unlikely to ever win plaudits for his contribution to fashion, Einstein hit upon a style that captured the popular imagination. Today, the flash of unkempt silver hair has become almost a shorthand for the lovable 'mad professor' type (one need only think of Doc Brown in the *Back to the Future* movies). Einstein's appearance even achieved the honour of featuring in a song that was popular among students at Princeton: 'The bright boys here all study Math / And Albie Einstein points the path / Although he seldom takes the air / We wish to God he'd cut his hair.'

Of course, to complete the Einstein look, you may also wish to adopt the 'tongue sticking out' pose so famously captured by photographer Arthur Sasse in 1951.

Don't Fight Time

'I have reached an age when, if someone tells
me to wear socks, I don't have to.'

ALBERT EINSTEIN

He may have been the man who redefined it, but Einstein came to realize that even he could not reverse time's passage. Like many people, he sporadically found the process of ageing painful and resented the resulting change in his treatment by others. Nonetheless, he adapted from 'young gun' to 'elder statesman' with considerable panache.

Einstein had always feared what old age might bring, especially in terms of diminishing intellectual capacities. Already by 1917, he was telling Heinrich Zangger that the really novel ideas were reserved for one's youth. Turning fifty pushed particular psychological buttons and by the time he was living permanently in the USA, he complained of feeling like a 'kind of ancient figure known primarily for his non-use of socks and wheeled out on special occasions as a curiosity'.

As a young scientist, Einstein had heroes hailing from throughout the ages. He said that the general theory, for instance, had its foundations in the work of four 'greats' in particular: Galileo, Newton, Maxwell and Lorentz. It was undoubtedly strange for him, then, to find that he was no longer the *wunderkind* standing on the shoulders of giants, but a giant himself. Where once he had built on and progressed the work of inspirational forefathers, others now stood upon his shoulders. In a few cases, including that of Max Planck, they had almost exchanged roles, Planck now using Einstein's work to refine his theory of quantum mechanics. 'To punish me for my contempt of authority,' he once said, 'Fate has made me an authority myself.'

In the course of this transformation, he also found himself no longer regarded as a scientific radical but rather a conservative, intent on upholding elements of classical physics while others were using products of his own theories (notably quantum mechanics) to dismantle them. Although he still considered himself working on the outer edges of physics, he was acutely aware of what others thought, poignantly confiding to Max Born in 1949: '… I am generally regarded as a sort of petrified object, rendered blind and deaf by the years.'

Naturally, adapting to these changing perceptions brought its frustrations, but in some aspects it was liberating. Rich enough and famous enough to pursue his own interests, the diminishing expectations of other people brought a sense of freedom – and not just in matters of sock-wearing. A 1954 letter to Queen Elisabeth of Belgium suggests he found sport in his run-ins with the US authorities over his anti-McCarthyist stance. He described himself as a 'kind of *enfant terrible* …

due to my inability to keep silent and swallow everything that happens'.

But it is in a continuation of his words to Born in 1949 where we can see best that Einstein took to old age rather well, accepting its challenges both gracefully and disgracefully:

I simply enjoy giving more than receiving in every respect, do not take myself nor the doings of the masses seriously, am not ashamed of my weaknesses and vices, and naturally take things as they come with equanimity and humour.

Make Your Peace with the Cosmos

'For us believing physicists, the distinction between past, present and future is only a stubborn illusion.'

ALBERT EINSTEIN, SPEAKING AFTER THE DEATH OF HIS FRIEND MICHELE BESSO IN 1955

As he faced the prospect of his own mortality, Einstein displayed remarkable calmness and fortitude. Though he could not lean on the traditional religious concept of an afterlife, he had spent his years examining the nature of time and matter, which rendered him nothing if not philosophical. Back in 1926, he had corresponded with the widow of Heike Kamerlingh Onnes, a Dutch physicist who had won the Nobel Prize in 1913, and reassured her: 'Our death is not an end if we can live on in our children and the younger generation. For they are us; our bodies are only wilted leaves on the tree of life.'

He was, at heart, a man more interested in the macro than the micro, always drawn more to the grand universal field theory than to sub-atomic quantum theory. A 'big picture' chap, as it were. Once, on being asked by the wife of an academic colleague how he maintained his levity in the face of the world's depravity, he replied: '… We must remember that this is a very small star, and probably some of the larger and more important stars may be very virtuous and happy.'

His adventures in science imbued him with a sense that he had somehow accessed a sort of immortality. 'People like you and I, though mortal of course, like everyone else, do not grow old no matter how long we live,' he told his friend, the psychologist Otto Juliusburger, in 1942. 'What I mean is that we never cease to stand like curious children before the great mystery into which we were born.' And in another letter to Queen Elisabeth in 1953, he wrote: 'The strange thing about growing old is that the intimate identification with the here and now is slowly lost; one feels transposed into infinity, more or less alone.'

Certainly, he had several years in which his own poor health and the deaths of others close to him served as ongoing reminders of mortality. Having lost Elsa in 1936, his first wife Mileva died in 1948 after a fall. That same year, Einstein himself was diagnosed with an aneurysm in his abdominal aorta and his beloved sister, Maja, was also seriously ill. In his last years, he built a number of bridges in his personal life, achieving rapprochement with his son, Hans Albert. It is also indicative of his mellowing that Maja and his stepdaughter Margot both chose to spend significantly more time with him in his final years than with their own husbands.

In 1955, he suffered a collapse related to his aneurysm. His loyal secretary, Helen Dukas, was deeply distraught as she saw his condition deteriorate. Einstein, though, exuded tranquillity. 'It is tasteless to prolong life artificially,' he told her. 'I have done my share, it is time to go. I will do it elegantly.' On 17 April he used up his last energies working on the theory of everything and died in the early hours of 18 April. His body was cremated (though his brain was embalmed and retained by Thomas Harvey, who carried out an autopsy at Princeton Hospital) and his ashes scattered in the Delaware River. Einstein was finally at one with the cosmos.

Some five years earlier, the *Observer* had quoted Einstein's ultimate equation, far more significant than even $E = mc^2$. 'If A is success in life, then A equals x plus y plus z. Work is x; y is play; and z is keeping your mouth shut.'

Five Things They Said About Einstein

'Through Albert Einstein's work the horizon of mankind has been immeasurably widened, at the same time as our world picture has attained a unity and harmony never dreamed of before.' – Niels Bohr

'Einstein would be one of the greatest theoretical physicists of all time even if he had not written a single line on relativity.' – Max Born

'Among twentieth-century men, he blends to an extraordinary degree those highly distilled powers of intellect, intuition, and imagination which are rarely combined in one mind, but which, when they do occur together, men call genius. It was all but inevitable that this genius should appear in the field of science, for twentieth-century civilization is first and foremost technological.' – Whittaker Chambers, writing in *Time*

'No other man contributed so much to the vast expansion of twentieth-century knowledge. Yet no other man was more modest … more sure that power without wisdom is deadly … Albert Einstein exemplified the mighty creative ability of the individual in a free society.' – President Dwight D. Eisenhower

'He is cheerful, assured, and courteous, understands as much of psychology as I do of physics, and so we had a pleasant chat.' – Sigmund Freud

Selected Bibliography

Aczel, Amir, *God's Equation: Einstein, Relativity and the Expanding Universe*, Piatkus Books (2000)

Calaprice, Alice (ed.), *The Ultimate Quotable Einstein*, Princeton University Press (2013)

Einstein, Albert, *Ideas and Opinions*, Souvenir Press (2012)

Einstein, Albert, *Out of My Later Years*, Philosophical Library (1950)

Einstein, Albert, *Relativity: The Special and the General Theory*, Methuen (1920)

Einstein, Albert, *The World as I See It*, Citadel Press Inc. (2006)

Fölsing, Albrecht, *Albert Einstein: A Biography*, Viking (1997)

Isaacson, Walter, *Einstein: His Life and Universe*, Pocket Books (2008)

Moszkowski, Alexander, *Einstein the Searcher: His work explained from dialogues with Einstein*, Dutton (1921)

Pais, Abraham, *Subtle Is the Lord: The Science and the Life of Albert Einstein*, OUP (2005)

Robinson, Andrew, *Einstein: A Hundred Years of Relativity*, Palazzo Editions (2010)

Viereck, G. S., *Glimpses of the Great*, Macauley (1930)